SOCIAL REVOLUTION
IN THE
NEW LATIN AMERICA

SOCIAL REVOLUTION
IN THE
NEW LATIN AMERICA

A CATHOLIC APPRAISAL

EDITED BY JOHN J. CONSIDINE, M.M.

FIDES PUBLISHERS, INC.
NOTRE DAME, INDIANA

Library of Congress Catalog Card Number: 65-28808

Prepared for publication under the sponsorship of the
CATHOLIC INTER-AMERICAN COOPERATION PROGRAM
(CICOP)
LATIN AMERICA BUREAU, N. C. W. C.

CONTENTS

INTRODUCTION

The most solemn and beautiful moment of the Second Annual National Conference of the Catholic Inter-American Cooperation Program came with the reading of the homily of Archbishop Helder Camara of Recife, Brazil, at the evening Bible Service.

"Lord," the Archbishop prayed, "make us love the Eucharist more and more in the man who is poor. May we recognize in the image of his misery the presence of your Son. Help us, for the love of this man who is poor, to wage a fight to the death against the causes of his poverty.

"These days of study present a panorama: unjust social structures in Latin America; grave social crises shaking the countries of the continent; a Social Revolution which everywhere imposes itself. Revolution, not in the meaning of armed and bloody revolt, but of rapid and substantial change.

"Woe be to all Christians if the lowly become convinced that the Church has abandoned them in this dark hour. They cannot but believe that religion is indeed the opium of the people and Christianity an ally of privilege and exploitation . . ."

The finest hour of the conference was the reading and the presentation in person by Archbishop Antonio Samore of the Vatican to Cardinal Cushing of the apostolic letter of Pope Paul VI recounting in detail His Holiness' satisfaction at the efforts of the Catholics of the United States to serve their confreres in Latin America.

"The perseverance, continuity and farseeing clarity which mark your labors," declared the Pontiff, "have had the effect of raising to 4,091 the ecclesiastical, religious and lay personnel from the United States now working in Latin America."

He thanked the U.S. bishops for loaning clergy from their dioceses for Latin America. "We praise and encourage the Religious communities of men and women," he went on to say, "which with perseverance and tenacity are gradually fulfilling the engagement undertaken at the Congress of Notre Dame, Indiana, in 1961 of offering the Church in Latin America a tithe of their total membership by 1970."

The papers delivered and the discussions which followed at the study sessions of the conference evidently were not only informing but partook as well of something charismatic. This was indicated in interesting fashion by the sentiments expressed by some among the score of Protestant observers at the conference.

Rev. David R. Hunter, deputy general secretary of the National Council of Churches, declared before departing, "I have had a shattering experience and I use the word shattering advisedly and from the depth of my soul. I think you know as well as I do that the great barrier that stands between you and me and my brethren is the presence of stereotypes. The Vatican Council shattered most of my stereotypes about Roman Catholics and this conference has shattered all the rest. And I can only say it's the most pleasant shattering experience I've ever had."

Doctor Eugene Smith, the executive secretary of the World Council of Churches, spoke in similar vein.

"This has been a rich and rare privilege at many points," he said. "I marvel at feeling so utterly at home. I know that in part this is because of the skill of Monsignor Gremillion's hospitality but it's also been the openness and the friendliness on the part of all of you.

"I am grateful for all that we've learned about Latin America. . . . Above all, I'm grateful for the unmistakable signs of the movement of the Holy Spirit with power in a Church where this can happen."

Probably the strongest factor for good both in the conference papers and in the discussions was the hard-headed optimism and buoyancy that eventually came through no matter how foreboding the portrait of the difficulties in Latin America. Archbishop Samore in his able address sounded a note in this direction which aptly reflects the view of the conference participants.

"I confess that spiritually I feel ill," said His Excellency, "when I hear the voices of prophets of doom foretell a dark religious and social future for Latin America. Such voices seem the moanings of men affected by a congenital tendency to gather only the negative aspects of human reality. . . . Thus they interpret every protest and every legitimate request as the cry of subverting revolt, ignorant or forgetful of the fact that renewal, adjustment and transformation are of the very essence of justice and even more so of Christian love."

Pope Paul VI in his message expresses an encouraging appreciation of the significance of CICOP.

"We have learned with pleasure," he declares, "that the United States Bishops' Committee for Latin America has recently established a movement: the Catholic Inter-American Cooperation Program (CICOP), which seeks by educational means to promote greater understanding of Latin America's peoples among the Catholic millions of the United States. We are happy to learn that this year, for the first time, many bishops are introducing this program into their dioceses, and many religious superiors are recommending it to their communities by advocating the observance of Catholic Inter-American Cooperation Week. Such a step should produce rich fruits of knowledge, warm friendship and Christian concern."

AN INDEX OF CONTRIBUTORS

BANDEIRA de Corvalho, (Miss) Marina, Rio de Janeiro, Brazil. Secretary General of MEB (Brazilian Adult Education Movement), Brazilian Director of UNDA (International Catholic Association for Radio and TV), Superintendent of ASAPRESS (Brazilian News Agency). Though a native of Rio, and hence an authentic "carioca," Miss Bandeira's excellent command of English early secured her posts at both the American and Indian Embassies. She studied social work two years in Rio and Lisbon before becoming Secretary General for the Social Action Secretariat of the National Conference of Brazilian Bishops.

CALDERA, Dr. Rafael, Caracas, Venezuela. President of the Christian Democratic Organization of America (ODCA); Secretary General of the Social Christian Party of Venezuela (COPEI). In 1964 he was COPEI candidate for President and finished second. Professor at Central University and Catholic University Andrés Bello in Caracas, author of books on labor law and international social justice.

DOHERTY, William C., Jr., Washington, D. C. Director of Social Projects for the American Institute of Free Labor Development (AIFLD), Washington, D. C. 1950–52 assigned Brussels with International Confederation of Free Trade Unions (ICFTU). 1952–62 inter-American representative of Postal Telephone Workers in Latin America; assigned Mexico and Brazil where three of his six children born. Since 1962 AIFLD director as above.

GUERRERO, Doctor Rodrigo, Cali, Colombia. Secretary for Latin America of Pax Romana. Degree from Universidad del Valle, Cali, 1962 as Doctor of Medicine. Active participant in international Catholic student congresses in Latin America and Europe since 1959.

HART, Dr. James A., Dean, College of Commerce, De Paul

University, Chicago. Graduate of Georgetown University; formerly dean School of Business Administration, Seton Hall University; member of faculties at Fordham, Manhattan, Creighton. Extensive business travel in Europe, Asia, Latin America. As practicing attorney in New York, specialized in foreign business matters. Member of business and academic associations.

HOUTART, L'Abbé François. Director, Centre de Recherches Socio-Religieuses, Louvain, Belgium. Graduate Louvain University. 1952–53 U.S. Government fellowship Indiana University and University of Chicago; 1953 guest professor University of Montreal; 1954 guest professor University of Buenos Aires; 1956 secretary general International Conference of Religious Sociology. Articles and books on socio-religious subjects. Author with Emile Pin of *The Church and the Latin American Revolution,* Sheed and Ward 1965.

JORDAN, Mr. Hugo. Director of Institute of Agrarian Promotion, Santiago, Chile. Mr. Jordan, in addition to playing a major role in the Bishops' Agrarian Reform Plan in Chile, is a student of economic reform throughout Latin America and a critic of certain methods of the Alliance for Progress.

LANDAZURI Ricketts, Juan Cardinal, Lima, Peru. His Eminence Cardinal Landázuri Ricketts is Archbishop of Lima and Primate of Perú. Born in Arequipa of an old Peruvian family, graduate of University of Arequipa, he became a Franciscan Friar and received his doctorate *summa cum laude* in Rome. Franciscan Provincial in Perú, he was chosen coadjutor bishop of Lima and successor to the see.

LARRAIN Errázuriz, Most Rev. Manuel, Bishop of Talca, Chile. A pioneer in continental thinking on problems of the Church in Latin America, he is currently President of Latin American Bishops' Council (Consejo Episcopal Latinoamericano, CELAM), established in 1956 with continental secretariat in Bogotá, Colombia.

McGRATH, C.S.C., Most Rev. Mark G., Bishop of Santiago de Veraguas, Panama. Born in Panama of U.S. parents, educated Notre Dame University and Rome as member of Congregation of the Holy Cross. Theologian of eminence; 10 years dean of theology at Catholic University, Santiago, Chile; member of Theological Commission of Ecumenical Council; CICOP Program Chairman.

OTERO, René, Washington, D. C. Officer of Inter-American Development Bank. Bolivian by birth, educated Notre Dame and Harvard Universities in law, political sciences, public administration. 1945–56 member Cooperative Services of joint U.S.-Bolivian technical assistance program (Point Four); 1957–60 secretary of National Council for Monetary Stabilization. With IDB since 1960. Long active in Bolivian Catholic Action; Knight of St. Sylvester.

PEREZ Ramírez, Rev. Gustavo, Bogotá, Colombia. Director of Colombian Institute for Social Development, Bogotá. M.A. in Social Philosophy Gregorian University; PhD. Sociology, Louvain University. Father Pérez began his career in the celebrated South Bogotá project. He was named by Cardinal Concha to establish the Center for Socio-Religious Research, now reorganized as the Colombian Institute for Social Development. FERES regional secretary for Latin America.

PEZZULLO, (Miss) Caroline, Brooklyn, New York. Executive Secretary, Commission for International Development, New York City. Social studies at St. John's University. National president YCW and experience in specialized Catholic action. Traveled considerably as UN representative of YCW, including extended contacts in Brazil. Since 1961 with Commission for International Development, a non-confessional organization serving popular social movements.

POBLETE Barth, S.J., Rev. Renato. Director of Centro de Investigación y Acción Social, Santiago, Chile. After graduation from Catholic University of Santiago obtained Doctorate in Sociology at Fordham University. Disciple of Padre Hurtado, S.J., Padre Poblete has contributed in a major degree to socio-economic studies of a group of specialists working with Father Roger Vekemans, S.J. Father Poblete's latest book: *Crisis Sacerdotal.*

RICHARDS, C. P., Rev. Pedro, Montevideo, Uruguay. National Moderator of the Christian Family Movement, Uruguay. Born Argentina, ordained member of Passionists 1940. Founded Christian Family Movement Buenos Aires 1948; continental secretary C.F.M. 1957, traveling seven times around continent in this post. Only Latin American member of Commission for Laity, Ecumenical Council. Former Superior and Provincial Consultor of Argentine Passionists.

RITTER, Joseph Cardinal, St. Louis, Missouri. Bishop and later Archbishop of Indianapolis before transfer to St. Louis. Pioneer in movement among U.S. bishops to loan diocesan clergy to Latin America. Member of Bishops' Committee for Latin America.

SAMPERIO G., Rev. Héctor, Mexico City. Coordinator, Escuela Radiofónica Veracruzana, Mexico City. Born in Pachuca, Mexico; educated Mexican Pontifical National Seminary, Montezuma, New Mexico; appointed to social secretariat Mexico City, 1953; studied rural social action University of Montreal, Canada 1956. Participant since in Mexican social and civic projects.

VEKEMANS Van Cauwelaert, S.J., Rev. Roger, Santiago, Chile. Co-Director of DESAL (Center for Social and Economic Development in Latin America). Born Brussels 1921. Louvain University degrees in Philosophy, Theology, Political and Social Science, Sociology. Additional Sociology degrees, Universities of Munster, Nijmegen and Paris. Founder of: 1—Center for Research and Social Action Roberto Bellarmino, Santiago; 2—Catholic Housing Movement (TECHO), Santiago; 3—Federation of Socio-Religious Research Institutes (FERES), Brussels; 4—School of Sociology, Catholic University of Santiago. Adviser and sponsor for numerous social and academic projects in Europe and Latin America.

WUST, Rev. Isaac Th. J., Bogotá, Colombia. Organizer of Department of Education, CELAM. Born Amsterdam, Netherlands. Licentiate in Political and Social Sciences, University of Louvain. To Colombia as member of College for Latin America, Louvain. Cooperator with Father Gustavo Pérez in Bogotá for Center for Social Research in Latin America studies (FERES) and book on Church in Colombia. Directed study on Catholic Education in Latin America 1963. Since 1964 preparing Department of Education for CELAM.

SECTION I

Socio-cultural Considerations

Latin America and the United States — a Social Confrontation

Abbé François Houtart

Confronted with the widely differing conditions of Latin American and North American society, many people wonder why such economic and social differences exist among people who are really neighbors. At times they form rather harsh judgments about one group or the other. Has not God equally endowed the two continents with natural resources? Were they not both discovered at the same time? Have they not both experienced a comparable growth of population? Did not both win independence at approximately the same time?

We shall gain a better understanding of the evolution of social structures in Latin America by comparing them with those of North America. Thus we clarify the resemblances and dissimilarities between the two societies which explain why they have developed along divergent lines. As an observer from Belgium I am not native to either continent but I am honored and happy to comply with the request to prepare this appraisal since I have a deep appreciation and sense of union with both cultures.

The fact that I am a foreigner to both will allow you all the more freedom to criticize my analysis.

It might be well to recall the present day social structure of Latin America but we shall leave this to chapters that follow. Let me mention in passing, despite the areas of modernity in the various Latin American countries and regions, the important problems faced by large rural masses living under sub-human conditions on the fringe of normal economic, social, political and cultural life. Great regions suffer the handicaps of a regime of landed property still largely based on the latifundia. Problems arise from the expansion of the large cities, veritable catch-basins of the miseries which follow from unbalanced demographic growth. A social and political oligarchy holding power in many countries brings woes. Adjustments are demanded by the rise of new social classes, influenced by the role the universities play in this process. Trouble flows from the exaggerated economic dependence of the continent on the relatively few industrially developed countries: It is obvious that this picture differs greatly from any sketch of the social conditions in the United States. It is extremely helpful to know the explanation.

I. *Colonial Society in Latin America and the United States*

LATIN AMERICA   In the southern continent, the Spanish conquest was less a matter of living space and land settlement than a great adventure led by a few remarkable personalities. These leaders often acted without mandate and outside any administrative control, but within the framework of a fundamental triple motivation: a religious urge which fitted into the framework of the recently achieved reconquest of Spain from the Moors; an economic urge pointed toward the acquisition of gold and silver, and a humanistic urge to create for men a new Golden Age. An example of this last, among others which might be cited, is to be found in the reductions of Paraguay.

Those far-ranging adventurers, the Conquistadores, within some thirty years took possession of an immense continent. In North America, conquest resulted in a high-handed occupation of the land. As one author declares, in North America "colonization preceded conquest," while in Latin

America, "conquest preceded colonization."

Although they kept in close touch with the organization of the colonies of "the Indies," the monarchs of Spain and Portugal were forced by circumstances of time and distance to allow a certain latitude to those actually in the new territories. This fact little by little led to the creation of a local society of which certain characteristics persist to the present day. At the end of the conquest four groups held power: the colonial aristocracy (heirs of the conquerors), colonial business interests, representatives of the Crown, the clergy.

THE COLONIAL ARISTOCRACY By force of arms the Conquistadores had carved out for themselves immense fiefs. They undertook to exploit these with the help of an enslaved population. They settled down among their possessions. From conquerors they became lords of the manor. Charles V ratified this situation by instituting the encomienda.

By royal authority the encomendero received a group of Indians. He put them to work and imposed various taxes on them. In return, he guaranteed to defend the territory. He assumed civil power. He evangelized the Indians confided to him. The encomienda system came to rest more and more on a basis of ownership of land. The source of such land might be confiscation, the sale of public domains, or gifts from the Crown for services rendered.

The encomienda soon disappeared, giving way to the hacienda, a large rural property. Theoretically the worker on a hacienda was free, but his indebtedness kept him in servitude. In the seventeenth century, the state favored the extension of landed property. It sold domains, legalized the possession of usurped lands. It instituted the regime of the mayorage, whereby the family heritage remained indivisible. Financiers, business men and mining companies acquired vast domains. The owner of a latifundia was not interested so much in productivity as in the social prestige and the power that land gave him. He lived in town, leaving the responsibility for the exploitation of his property in the hands

of a manager. He leased or granted plots of land to the ex-
propriated Indians. The latter, in exchange for a bit of land
reserved to their own use, worked without pay for a certain
number of days a year. Despite these various dispositions, a
large part of the lands lay fallow. In Brazil, the fazenda (the
equivalent to hacienda) and especially the sugar plantations
represented a somewhat different social structure because
the fazendero usually lived on his land. In other respects the
same situations existed as in Spanish America.

It is important to note that the latifundia produced little.
The landed aristocracy was not interested in their exploitation, lacked a spirit of enterprise, and looked down on new
types of work. This agrarian structure, this disdain for work
which retarded economic development, are traits which still
characterize certain rural areas of many Latin American
countries.

THE COLONIAL BUSINESS INTERESTS A feudal system remained,
but capitalism was developing side by side with it. The slave
trade favored the accumulation of wealth. Thanks to credit,
financial capitalism predominated. Production was devoted
to trade, to the satisfaction of the needs of Spain.

Mines, tropical plantations and flour mills formed the
basis of Latin American business enterprise. The gold and
silver mines especially facilitated the development of Western capitalism and the industrialization of Europe, but in
Latin America itself they did not give rise to an industrial
middle class. Revenues from the mines permitted the importation of slaves and of manufactured products. They
made it possible to beautify the cities and fostered cultural
flowering. They did not develop a local industry, except
that of silk and leather. This was to the advantage of the
Crown, which was thus able to avoid a colonial competition
which would have ruined the home industries.

Colonial capitalism took on a commercial form, which
would remain after Latin American independence was won.
Side by side with the property owners, the business men

wielded great economic power. Lacking an expansion of credit, they associated themselves with the bankers. They controlled the coastwise trade. Thanks to mortgages, they held a number of rural properties.

THE COLONIAL ADMINISTRATION The third influential group was the colonial administration, strongly centralized from 1550 on. At the beginning, public offices were an honor, a reward. They became the prerogative of a salaried bureaucracy. The mother country itself directed colonial affairs through the Council of the Indies, supreme legislative and administrative organ. In America the Viceroy, or the Captain General in the captaincies, exercised royal power with the council of the Viceroy, the audiencia, which held administrative and judiciary powers.

The Crown established a service of functionaries with limited terms of office. The organization was strict but slow and costly. According to Pierre Chaunu it absorbed 50% of the revenues from the Indies in the sixteenth century, and 80% in the eighteenth century. Corruption eventually poisoned the administration. The functionary of the eighteenth century became "a business man who capitalized on his office and used for his own profit a good part of the revenues of the State."

The multiplication of public offices resulted in political decentralization. At the end of the eighteenth century, the Bourbons undertook an administrative reform with the creation of the intendancies. But it was already too late. The creoles (Spaniards born in Latin America), everywhere deprived of opportunity, were to become the rebels of the future.

The basis of economic policy was monopoly. *La Casa de Contratación* controlled all sea traffic and directed it at first to the port of Seville. In 1717 this city lost its commercial privileges to Cádiz. From 1717 to 1765, this latter port was the only place for trade. This centralization facilitated the control over gold and other precious metals and over the quinto (the fifth), the tax which the Crown levied on mining resources.

But Spain was eventually to lose her monopoly of trade with the Indies. For protection, her ships were soon forced to travel in convoy, and nevertheless treasures disappeared as a result of pirate raids. By the end of the eighteenth century other countries took charge of commerce between America and Europe. The French, Genovese, Dutch, English and Germans eventually handled 90% of exported capital.

Smuggling, fostered by rigid trade restrictions, the suppression of commerce from all ports except Panama, and prohibitive prices to European buyers, undermined the monopoly. The suppression of commerce from regional ports led to the appearance of independent economic operations which were later to contribute to political division. Restraint of commerce and corrupt administration brought on eventual collapse.

THE CLERGY Besides the great landed proprietors, the capitalists, and the royal administrative officers (three groups who exercised power or held real authority during the colonial period) a fourth group must be considered, the clergy. During this period the regular clergy, like the secular clergy, became quite wealthy and formed at the end of the colonial period an important economic power. They possessed immense properties as a result of gifts, inheritances, privileges and mortgages. The immovable capital of the Church often enough represented only a small productive value. One exception in this regard is the case of the Jesuits, who were great producers, setting up models of administration and of capitalist technique. These properties served generally to assure the financial basis of educational and religious activities.

THE SOCIAL SITUATION We have seen now how the economic, social, political and cultural power was shared. But what was the social situation? Great geographical as well as cultural distances separated the various ethnic groups.

The hierarchy of classes had feudal and economic bases. As concerned the feudal, the conquerors, privileged by the Crown, became encomenderos or lords. The landed proprietors assumed power at the same time as the government functionaries and the wealthy businessmen. The stratification sprang less from a concern for a feudal system than from a desire to conserve acquired economic privileges. By the seventeenth century the crystallization of society into colonial castes was an accomplished fact.

Population growth and the increase of intermarriage between the Spanish-born, the creole, the Indian and the Negro proved to be factors of social mobility which overthrew the principle of separation on which the colonial system originally rested.

The figure of the pyramid shows this social hierarchy clearly. At the top: the Spaniards. At the base: the Negroes and the Indians. Between the top and the base, and going up from bottom to top, the mulattos, the Indian half-breeds, and finally the "mestizos" of Spanish culture.

At the very top of the pyramid stood the whites, the Spaniards of Spain. They monopolized the higher posts in administration and in the Church. The creoles were ousted. Aside from the higher officials and the upper clergy, birth and family position based on the ownership of lands and mines determined rank. The prestige attached to birth and to property and the disdain for commercial enterprises however lucrative placed business men and those engaged in industry in an inferior social rank in spite of their economic power.

At the base of the pyramid came the slave or paid laborer, excluded from the political and cultural life of the nation. Included in this lowest stratum were the Indians enrolled in the encomiendas, then subject to the forced labor of the mita and later linked with the haciendas. The Indians formed the urban and rural proletariat. The change from one system to another (encomienda, hacienda or mita) did not improve the social condition of the Indians, each of the systems serving only to reduce them to a still lower level.

At the beginning of colonization, a few noble Indians retained rank and prestige when they were hispanicized. There were also a few attempts at indirect administration, through the intermediary of the cacique, or head man. Under the authority of the encomendero, the caciques served as recruiting agents and collected taxes. Caciques who were too solicitous for the interests of the Indians were removed and replaced by men less friendly toward their own.

The Indian population as a whole was cut off from the new society who were mostly city dwellers. The Indian had no normal access to the new social or cultural order.

However, it is important to note that if the structuring of society followed strongly marked lines of ethnic and cultural separation, neither the Spaniard nor the Portuguese disdained racial mixtures. Quite generally illegitimate, unions between persons of different races were frequent at all levels of society.

On the sides of the population pyramid we should find the middle classes. For practical purposes we can say that they did not exist. Groups of mestizos, who by their geographic location (in towns) and their occupations (small artisans or business men) should have been separate from the lower level, remained linked to it because of their poverty and their illiteracy.

Little by little certain mestizos entered into competition with some elements of society as merchants, artisans or small proprietors. They were usually impoverished vagrants who formed the group of poor whites. This intermediate group did not evolve toward the middle class until the very end of the colonial period. Its rise had been impeded by the social system and by a whole series of economic restraints. This class found it impossible to acquire a small property, they were restricted in the purchase of manufactured goods. They were lost in the lower strata of society and could not rise.

Parallel to this rigid structuring, geographic and cultural barriers separated the ethnic groups. Parts of the aboriginal populations, for instance the jungle Indians, lived "outside" colonial society. Their remoteness was not always due to the fact of distance. It often resulted from a withdrawal in the face of conquest, as was the case of several groups of Guaranís in Paraguay after the destruction of their villages. Also, some populations, such as the Indians of the reductions and the communities, were and still are living in relative cultural and social independence, though by their acceptance of Christianity they have experienced an acculturation, at least in the religious domain.

As to the independence of the Indian, it has always been of very precarious nature. Their reductions were in effect but refuges for a very poor population, victims of land speculation and subject to the servitude of the mita. The Christian republic established by the Jesuits in the Paraguay reductions, sometimes characterized as Communist Christian, attempted an economic, social, cultural and religious integration. After the suppression of the Society the reductions came to a tragic end, due in part to the inability of its directors to make progress beyond the paternalistic character of the experiment.

Sergio Bagu in his study of social structures of colonial Latin America notes the existence of a considerable population of non-producers, of persons who had lost social position, more or less permanently unemployed, living by their wits and by occasional favors. This group included the great mass of mestizos, of Negroes and fugitive Indians. Turned out of their communities or desirous of escaping forced labor, these men constituted the marginal groups of the cities.

SOCIAL STRUCTURES IN NORTH AMERICA Class distinctions also appeared in what is now the United States during the colonial period. It is important, however, to make a distinction between the social structuring of the Northern colonies and those of the Southern colonies because they present quite different characteristics.

Following the landing of the Mayflower, the Pilgrims (separatists from the Anglican Church) formed an independent colony. Since the reasons which led them to emigrate were essentially religious, the first social leaders were the ministers, and the whole social life was subordinated to the prescriptions of the Church. Social organization rested on two principles: on the one hand collective administration, and on the other, the division of the land into equal parts. Since there were no great landed properties there would be no feudal privileges. These two principles contributed to forge that democratic spirit which is still present in the America of today.

In contrast to what happened in Latin America, the first North American society did not know racial mixture. Practically as a consequence of this, the native population was almost completely destroyed or pushed into "reserves" where it lost a real social existence in the new society. It is true that the Indian population within what is now the United States was not as numerous as in Latin America and lacked examples of cultural advance, such as Latin America's Inca and Mayan civilizations.

North American society was formed by settlers of humble origin, later joined by small merchants and indentured servants (plebian and sometimes delinquent elements whose work was to cover the expenses of their emigration and who were to form the first proletariat). All were animated by the same ambition, that of the English middle class ideal, that is, the possession of one's own independent means of existence.

Later on, leadership rested on other bases. The leaders were those who had ambition and ability and who were able to compel recognition. An upper class began to take shape; its prestige rested on the money accumulated through commerce, including the slave trade. Eventually these leaders constituted an oligarchy of powerful merchants. A mercantile class formed of tradesmen, ship builders and others also developed. But the great proportion of the population lived by agriculture. Except for servants and slaves, all were owners of their property.

So much for the northern colonies of North America. The situation in the southern colonies was more like that in Latin America. Driven out of England by Cromwell or impelled by the taste for adventure, the first migrants were of higher social origin than that of the northerners. Patterning their style of living on that of the English aristocracy, they took for themselves huge properties whose exploitation was to require the very large African labor force which they proceeded to build up. Southern society, like that in Latin America, was thus divided into two strata.

The upper stratum, formed by English settlers, included several categories of families, determined according to birth. Slavery soon effected an important distinction between them. The social hierarchy was based on the number of slaves each person owned. Nevertheless, and here the comparison with Latin America is no longer valid, although manual work was judged degrading, the value accorded the land depended on both its extent and its productivity.

Note here, and this is equally true for both North and South, that we are scarcely mentioning industry. England, like Spain and Portugal, considered its colonies as furnishers of raw materials and discouraged all attempts at development in this domain. This policy, incidentally, further increased the wealth of the south, producer of cotton, tobacco and sugar. In prerevolutionary days there was very little contact between the two colonial groups principally because of the difficulty of north-south communication. Most colonies were served by rivers which flowed west to east.

II. *Significance of Independence in Latin America and in the United States*

At the end of the eighteenth century, the entire Western Hemisphere was shaken by a desire for independence. Everywhere colonial rule was rejected. From our point of view today, what did this new situation mean?

INDEPENDENCE IN LATIN AMERICA   Although Latin America was open to modern ideas, political revolutions were unleashed when Latin America did not have the social background of European countries or of the United States. Spanish authoritarianism did not favor political education any more that it did the exercise of the spirit of enterprise or of economic freedom. The social structure remained quite undemocratic, based on privilege and caste.

While in the European countries and in North America revolutions profited the already rich and well organized middle classes, permitted their expansion and brought them to political power, in Latin America they did not serve such a function. The system of monopoly prevented the exercise of economic liberties and stifled the spirit of initiative. It gave rise to regional autarchy.

At the time of independence this led to the breaking up of the former Spanish colonies. Brazil succeeded in remaining united, because with the outbreak of revolution in Portugal the king settled in his Brazilian colony, establishing a monarchy which lasted until 1889. While in the United States the union of the various states was progressively established, in Latin America the movement was in the opposite direction. New divisions appeared throughout the nineteenth century, to such a point that at the end of the Spanish colonial regime, there were eighteen republics.

SOCIAL AND POLITICAL ASPECTS   Latin America's revolutions were directed at the political and economic power of the mother country just as in the United States, but the basic social structure was completely different. Feudal type local oligarchies became even more solidly entrenched in power through the break with Spain.

Like the United States and France, Latin America wrote liberal constitutions, but without a basis in its social structure capable of guaranteeing them. Latin America likewise lacked the technical means that might permit her to establish her economic independence in the jungle of political expansion. Thus the revolutions were political without being social. This particular social situation and the virulence of centrifugal forces—the feudal caudillismo of the landed proprietors and of the military leaders—brought to power new independent regimes, oligarchies or dictatorships.

As Leopold Zea puts it: "The conservative forces were so powerful that they were quite able to make use of the possibilities offered by a democratic regime to destroy liberties, and the liberal forces wore themselves out in multiple political struggles against their enemies and among themselves to the detriment of the other condition indispensable to the strength of the nation: material progress and well-being. Faced with the danger that conservative action represents in a democratic regime whose institutions the conservatives use to overthrow it, and faced also with a pitiful material stagnation, it was easy to fall into the opposite extreme, into dictatorships called 'dictatorships for freedom.'

"In the history of our country these latter were a necessary step toward the formation of the nucleus of nationhood. But the dictatorships, forgetting the end for which they had been created, became purely and simply dictatorships for the protection of the interests of a particular social group."[1]

Lacking the social and cultural foundations which permit the establishment of a democracy, the countries of Latin America went through a series of enlightened dictatorships and oligarchic governments. These minorities, sometimes interested in the progress of the nation, theoretically represented the people but they found their justification not so much in the will of the governed as in the national betterment which it was so urgent for their nations to actualize.

---

[1] L. Zea, "l'Amerique hispanique et le monde occidental," *Esprit*, No. 10, Oct. 1958, pp. 482–483.

These dictatorships, described as democratic caesarism, restricted liberties and thus were not able to provide an apprenticeship for democracy nor to give the people the means of achieving democracy. They were interrupted by military dictatorships, representing private interests. From the second half of the nineteenth century, these regimes often served foreign economic powers.

LATIN AMERICA'S ECONOMY   Indeed, Latin America found itself at grips with the expansionist policies of the Western nations. It was not only a question of military or political expansionism. It became very soon a region of foreign investments and served as a veritable financial and commercial colony, first of European then of North American capitalism.

This economic role of Latin America certainly did not promote its development. Neither did the fact that during the colonial period the conception of a destructive economy had prevailed. This economy led rather to the exhausting of natural resources than to their full utilization. The desire for easy wealth, unaccompanied by any spirit of enterprise or appreciation of the value of work, developed in the Latin American countries a spirit of individualistic speculation, lacking any national outlook.

With independence the social groups of the colonial period were slightly modified. The administration of the mother country had in fact been ousted, but there remained the landed oligarchy and commercial capitalism. Further, the lot of the marginal masses had not been basically changed. An intermediate class did not get established, except to a slight extent through political means. Foreigners, Europeans and North Americans, exercised an important role in the economic functions.

At the end of the nineteenth century and during the first part of the twentieth, a large number of Europeans immigrated to Latin America. But the countries they chose were those of the southern zone: Argentina, Uruguay and Chile, as well as the south of Brazil. In the three first-mentioned countries they settled in the cities and formed the basis of the present middle class, more developed than elsewhere in these nations, while in Brazil, it was above all a question of rural settlements.

During the nineteenth century the social structures remained fairly fixed. The principal influences were the following: 1) rather numerous but quite superficial political changes; 2) the birth of the republic of Brazil, its regime based on models quite like those of the other countries; 3) breakups and internal struggles: Uruguay, Central America, Greater Colombia, wars between Chile and Peru; 4) the manifestation of certain foreign designs: those of the United States on Mexico and Panama, of the United Kingdom on Venezuela, of France on Mexico.

THE INTRODUCTION OF CHANGE   It was at the beginning of the twentieth century that the first elements of a transformation began to take form in the north and south of Latin America. In Mexico there was the revolution of 1917 and the socialist type regimes which succeeded each other after 1917. In Argentina the industrialization of Buenos Aires had its beginning. These two movements were to usher in agrarian reform. In Mexico the *ejidos,* a form of collective property, played a role. In Argentina at a later date came peronism.

In the twentieth century the demographic expansion began. There were 63 million inhabitants in 1900 and 131 million in 1940. Then came the population explosion which was to result in 163 million in 1950, more than 200 million in 1960, and about 225 million at the present time. In 1900 the United States had 66 million inhabitants, practically the equivalent of all Latin America, and has reached only 183 million today.[2]

---

[2] Since the year 1900, Latin America has increased in population by 355% and the United States 277%.

A few social movements arose, but very sporadically, before the Second World War. These movements gave an impetus to military or civil dictatorships attributed to interest in the rural or urban masses. Communications were improved and quickly lessened the cultural isolation of the marginal populations.

But despite such movements and several revolutions, such as that of Bolivia in 1952, social structures have remained rigid. A break with the *ancien regime* has not yet been made, except perhaps in Cuba. However, radical social change would appear to be a *sine qua non* of development. The population explosion makes it imperative. Improved communications and the mass media have drawn the marginal masses out of their isolation and created an increasing social consciousness. The need for an accelerated economic growth requires that the Latin American peoples be masters of their own economic decisions and less dependent on outside help. This situation has prepared the crisis of which more will be said later.

THE CHURCH IN LATIN AMERICA The Catholic Church, still the majority religion, is in a very difficult situation. She too has suffered from the revolutions in the measure in which she was, at least in her hierarchy, an expression of the power of the mother country. Besides, the wealthy classes coveted the property of the Church which was confiscated. Liberal ideologies, the regalism prevalent in Brazil, controversies over the right of patronage which the new republics claimed as a heritage created politico-religious conflicts which prevented the Church from developing her structures. Thus her seminaries, parishes, convents and schools have suffered. The social revolutions of the twentieth century quickly took on anti-religious aspects. One thinks of Mexico.

From all this followed quasi-permanent conflicts between the State and the Church in all but a few Latin American countries. A great number of Catholics, particularly the clerics, possess nothing better as a point of reference than the *ancien regime*. Hence Latin America's Church leaders often saw their future only in the light of the Church's past. They contented themselves with condemning liberalism, referring to religion's former glories and seeking support in conservative parties.

However, within the last twenty years or so a profound change has taken place. In several countries the hierarchy has taken the leadership in social transformation, by sound declarations, by good example in social initiatives of its own and by strong moral support of governmental social programs. In the face of such a disfunctional role in regard to existing social structures and of attitudes which often favor social revolution, some have become frightened, even in the Church. Thus one of the elements in the current crisis is a danger of the creation of rather new and aggressive conservative fronts.

INDEPENDENCE IN THE UNITED STATES   In the United States, independence had a different meaning. The war of 1812 and the Napoleonic blockade made the development of local industry indispensable. Besides, the improvement of communications permitted massive immigrations from Europe and facilitated internal commerce and trade.

The difficulties of all kinds which the immigrants encountered on their way westward prompted many to settle in the cities. Thus, in addition to peopling the vast hinterland they swelled the ranks of the urban industrial population. It was the boom period for such cities as Buffalo, Chicago and Cleveland.

With ample manpower, freed from economic dependence on England, well supplied with both raw materials and capital, culturally anglo-saxon, North America embarked on the road to economic prosperity. Rugged individualism was the catch phrase that inspired vigor and courage but solid social structures took form as well.

It was at this time that the Civil War broke out, really a

result of the socio-economic imbalance existing between the U.S. North and the U.S. South. The defeat of the South marked the progressive disappearance of the slave-centered social system prevailing there. Racial segregation, however, was to remain as a witness to the slavery that had been, and was to influence the whole of American society.

After the Civil War, industrial development was prodigious. If the process was parallel to that of Europe, it was much more rapid. No out-worn institution held back any longer the rise of the modern economic structure. However, the rapid transition from an agrarian economy to an industrial economy of production was not made without difficulties and conflicts. A deepening chasm yawned between capitalists and the working class, while capital tended to concentrate more and more in the hands of a few. By 1910, control of business was focused within the domain of the railroads, steel, sugar and copper.

This situation struck at the heart of the middle class. Independent businesses were reduced to insignificance by the economic activity of the trusts. At the beginning of the 19th century, small businesses represented four-fifths of the active population, in 1870 one third, in 1940 one fifth.

It took the New Deal to redress the balance. For onlookers throughout the world, the capacity of the U.S. political leaders to rectify the deep social and economic problems of this nation by the ordered legislation of the New Deal was an amazing triumph for the democratic process.

New employment opportunities developed in such areas as administration and commerce. As the economic functions of the nation grew they produced in their turn a cultural and social order leading to a growing complexity of the social organism and to the progressive enlargement of the American middle class.

In the United States, history has moved in the direction of an ever-increasing differentiation of functions, of a proportionate decrease in the number of manual workers, and of an increase in semi-skilled and white collar workers.

THE U.S. CHURCH The Catholic Church was present in the United States before independence. It was a minority church and was sometimes even persecuted. Yet the liberal constitution of the United States was not only supported by Catholics, but was in good part promulgated thanks to their action, since it guaranteed religious liberty. It was with immigration, however, that the Catholic Church achieved its great numerical expansion. With Catholic ranks made up for the most part of immigrants of the working class whose natural spokesman was the Church, the Church has been identified from early days with their struggle for social justice, even if some priests and bishops did not always favor unionism.

Since the Second World War especially, the Catholic population has formed an important part of the lower and upper middle classes. The former place in the immigrant worker group occupied by European Catholics is now assumed by Negroes, Puerto Ricans and Mexicans not accompanied by their own clergy. Many U.S. Catholics no longer identify themselves with the poor. It is therefore not surprising that a wave of conservatism has swept over a segment of the clergy and Catholics of the United States, making it sometimes difficult for them to understand the more progressive attitude of some Latin Americans on socioeconomic questions.

From this analysis I should like now to draw out the main lines which seem to me to explain why today we find ourselves face to face with such different situations in the two parts of the Western Hemisphere. They are at once geographical, cultural, social, political and economic.

III. *Latin America and the United States, a confrontation*

GEOGRAPHIC DIFFERENCES The geography and the climate of the two continents are quite diverse. A much greater portion of Latin America's population dwells in tropical and

subtropical climates which create very different conditions
for work and development. North America's major river
basin, the Mississippi, fits far more felicitously into the living plan than does South America's, the Amazon basin.
Many U.S. geographic factors have helped a great deal,
economically and socially, in the integration of this part of
the hemisphere. A great deal of Latin America's mining
resources are located in almost inaccessible places. Coal and
iron, so abundant and handy to each other in North America, favored the first period of industrial revolution, while
in Latin America they do not exist in the same proportion
and seldom are conveniently close to each other.

CULTURAL DIFFERENCES   From the colonial period, marked
differences are found in the value systems animating the
settlers of the United States and of Latin America. The
English origin of the former oriented the type of colonization from the beginning. The individual's will to work and
the capacities which he brought with him were among the
fundamental differences. In the case of most North American immigrants, the traditions of their origin led men toward research, invention, the perfection of the tools of production and the consequent technical civilization. While
many settlers in the southern states of the United States
possessed different values originally, they came eventually
into the "Yankee" orbit. True, this accentuated economic
development and thus tended to create a society concerned
overwhelmingly with material achievement. Sometimes this
works a hardship on the deeper instincts of the individual
man.

In Latin America, Spanish aristocratic society saw little
value in work and production and placed emphasis rather
on unproductive wealth as a yardstick of social status.
There was often concern for the disinterested expression of
culture, influencing notably the very structure of society itself. It suffices to compare the colonial regime of farm property in what later became the northern United States with

the haciendas of the Spanish and Portuguese colonies.

All of this was related to a more profound philosophical attitude toward life. A negative approach toward the world and what today we would call development resulted from a cyclical conception of time as opposed to duration and to a real vision of the future. This was encouraged by the concept of life as essentially a preparation for death. Later the waves of immigration would seem to have taken this difference in the way of life into account, the Northern and Central Europeans going to the United States and Canada, and the Mediterranean peoples going to South America. Whether or not many actually made the choice on the head of this difference, the two divergent trends only accentuated the already existing situation.

SOCIAL DIFFERENCES There are clearly defined differences in the way the two societies are structured. Let us remark that in the United States, the original Indian population played no role because it was exterminated or driven out. Later, society was structured according to individual possessions or ability and scarcely at all according to the prestige of birth. There was great social mobility from the very beginning. Industrialization certainly influenced the social structure, but the democratic spirit of the early days survived nourished by the successive waves of immigrants who wished to earn money, get an education at least for their children, become completely assimilated and thus rise quickly to the higher status of this new society.

In Latin America, the existence of aboriginal populations called for meeting the situation in different terms. Social stratification was largely determined by race. The European element formed the elite, while the colored or the assimilated populations (the Brazilian *sertao* for example) made up the masses. It is easy to understand that in such a situation social mobility was in the earlier period practically non-existent. Although this division was mitigated later by intermarriage, it has strongly marked the Latin

American social evolution. The absence of industrial development and the prolonged colonial economy fostered the rigidity of undifferentiated social structures.

POLITICAL DIFFERENCES   The political systems of colonization were also quite dissimilar. In the North, the emigres formed relatively independent colonies, British tutelage being more economic than political. There resulted from this a certain political apprenticeship, which was to find natural expression in the new situation of independence.

In Latin America, on the contrary, Spanish authoritarianism implanted itself with its entire organization. After independence, the new governments in spite of their liberal constitutions maintained very similar systems, without integrating the masses into political life.

ECONOMIC DIFFERENCES   We have already said that the value system oriented the North Americans toward economic development. One could say that industrialization was the fruit of a logical evolution.

In Latin America, this was not the case. Industrialization was introduced from without, and for this reason did not have a balanced development. In spite of political independence, the continent lives today in an economy based essentially on the primary sector (mining and agriculture), since it serves as a reservoir for industrialized countries.

The secondary sector (industry) is relatively undeveloped. On the other hand, the tertiary sector which should have flowed from the development of the secondary has reached enormous proportions in urban milieux. But this is only the result of the population surplus coming from the rural areas, where development has been arrested because of social immobility.

These considerations on the differences between the two parts of the hemisphere help us to understand two very important facts. The first one is the essential need of profound structural changes in Latin America. It is not too strong to speak about "social revolution"—a concept which does not inevitably imply violence—because a rupture with the *ancien regime* is a *sine qua non* for development. This need is based on deep historical roots; it cannot be met merely by a moralistic approach. Structural changes are requisite.

The second fact is Latin America's need to abandon faulty social, economic and cultural ideologies. Faulty ideology has played and still plays a much greater role in Latin America than it has in North America. We may not, of course, reduce Christianity to an ideology, but we cannot insist too much with Christians that they recognize the spiritual and cultural arguments for social change and development.

Here you have then, briefly and with a certain over-simplification of some of the phases, a comparative appraisal of the two societies. May it help us to understand better the problems with which Christians of Latin America are at present confronted. It may also help to clarify the problems which Christians of the United States encounter in their dialogue with their brothers to the South.

CHAPTER 2

The Social Crisis in Latin America

Roger Vekemans, S.J.

Latin America, does it exist or not? We cannot enter into that discussion, which is a very complex one, but when we talk about Latin America as a whole, as a unit, we certainly should never forget that it's a highly heterogeneous continent. Any indicator we may want to use to describe the continent whether it be an economic one like, let's say, yearly per capita income, or a social one like the number of hospital beds per 10,000 inhabitants, those indicators would always oscillate ten times more in Latin America than within, let's say, Western Europe. So when we talk about Latin America, let us never forget that to some extent we are talking about an abstraction, and that the unit is essentially highly differentiated.

A second remark concerns the term social. In the context of this topic I would like to use the word social in its broad sense in which it embraces all the possible dimensions of the global social phenomenon, the economic one, the demographic one, the anthropological one, the cultural one, the political one, and so on. It will not refer to the social crisis exclusively in, let's say, sociological terms of social stratification, social mobility, social change.

And finally the word crisis. In this case I would like to take the word crisis in two different meanings. One, crisis as a rupture point within a given evolution, which is a quite obvious meaning of the word. And the other one, the etymological sense of the word crisis, namely judgment, consciousness, awareness. I think both meanings apply to our problem.

FIRST STEP, THE ECONOMIC APPROACH   To approach our topic I would propose a rather superficial first step, namely the economic one. I majored in sociology so in my opinion economics is mainly superficial. Let us therefore take as a first step the economic approach.

As you know, one of the main theses of the Economic Commission for Latin America of the United Nations says that the main trouble with Latin America is the fact that within the world's economy-labor division, Latin America has been appointed as a major producer of raw materials. Latin America has been reduced to the primary sector of the economy. Over the last fifty years, this fact has brought about a very deep economic crisis in Latin America. A crisis called again by the Economic Commission for Latin America the crisis of the deterioration of the terms of trade.

The exogenous direction of the Latin American economy explains its weakness, and even in many cases the fact that the Latin American economy as a whole is progressing so slowly. It explains also in the opinion of the economic commission why Latin America still stays at a rather low technological level, why its population is characterized by poor skill. It explains why, since it is a continent basically dedicated to agriculture (over 50%) and mining, the area's few industrial activities are characterized by rather high and intensive concentration on extraction of raw materials, as in the case of copper in Chile, and rather poor capacity for manpower absorption. This latter explains the unemployment, real or disguised, and therefore, because the labor market is so weak, the weakness of the labor movement as a motor of social progress.

THE DRAMATIC IMBALANCE   Taking this as a starting point, and taking into account the other basic fact of the population explosion in Latin America (everybody knows today that Latin America has the highest birth rate in the world and therefore also the highest population growth of the world today), it's quite understandable that we get to a rather dramatic imbalance between population, on the one hand, and available resources, services and goods, on the other. Or in more dynamic terms, the dramatic imbalance today between the population growth on the one hand, and the economic expansion on the other.

These are rather obvious facts known and accepted to some extent by almost everybody. Still, we should point out that this thesis, which could be called a basic one, has to be taken with some grains of salt because it is applied to almost every underdeveloped continent, including to some extent Africa and Asia. Yet the famous United Nations stereotype of Africa, Asia, Latin America is certainly basically wrong. Latin America although really underdeveloped, although poor because of this imbalance between economic development and population growth, because of the scarcity of resources available for today's population is nevertheless a middle class continent compared to Africa and Asia.

ECONOMICALLY MIDDLE CLASS   We cannot say of Latin America, as it has been said, that it is a proletariat continent. Take whatever indicator you like, for instance, the synthetic one from the point of view of economics, the per capita yearly income, and for Latin America you'll get a level of about $400 yearly per capita. For the continents of Africa and Asia, the per capita yearly income amounts to $100. This means that if you compare Latin America with the underdeveloped continents you get almost four times the per capita income of Asia and Africa and only three times less than the average Western European per capita income.

Thus, if it is true that Latin America is an underdeveloped continent, still we have to take into account that it possesses a starting point for growth above that of other underdeveloped areas of the world. This is true not only from the economic point of view but also in a broader sense, for instance that of culture. Economically speaking, we should say, I think, that Latin America is a middle class continent and culturally I would say it should be termed an area of the Western world although of highly mixed population. These are characteristics which have to be taken into account.

Taking into account this remark about the existence of several levels of underdevelopment, let's get closer to the point of our topic and consider some typically social consequences of this starting point. Let's note another obvious factor—the ecological imbalance within Latin America.

DICHOTOMY BETWEEN URBAN AND RURAL   Everybody recognizes the dichotomy between urban and rural. But in Latin America it takes on an image which is much more dramatic than anywhere else. It's difficult to talk about one Latin America, as I've already said. There are 20 countries and we should talk about 20 countries because they really are different one from another. But if we want to make one basic generalization about the area we should talk about the one Latin America of the urban belt along the coast.

When you come, let's say, from Europe you stop in Rio, Sao Paulo, Montevideo, Buenos Aires, Santiago, Lima. You've gone on and on and yet practically speaking you've never left the urban belt of Latin America which possesses a level of living which we could call average European.

But once you leave that urban belt along the coast, you get into the interior, the hinterland where some three/fourths of the Latin American population dwells. This vast rural area of the continent is farther behind the urban belt than the urban belt in turn is behind Europe. This we should never forget.

And there we have in my opinion the typical projection of what must be said about the Latin American problem as regards terms of trade. Latin Americans can well complain about the deterioration of their terms of trade when they talk about the selling of the raw materials on the international markets. But within each country we have exactly the same problem. Within Latin America today the gap between the general culture of the rural areas and the urban belt is getting wider and wider just as the gap steadily grows between underdeveloped continents and developed continents of the globe.

THE RURAL INVASION   The disintegration problem, which currently plays a big role in world solidarity, can be verified as well within Latin America as a whole and within each of the Latin American countries. From the ecological point of view, a major factor in breaking the dichotomy between rural and urban areas of Latin America constitutes today one of the most dramatic colonizations going on anywhere on the planet. I refer to the invasion of the urban belt by the rural population. In every country of Latin America there is a steady build-up of marginal populations within the urban belt, an emigration from the underdeveloped rural areas to the centers of modernization within the urban belt. The name of these settlements is different in each country but the reality is basically the same. We have a red belt (most of the time it's red) of suburban population around each one of our cities which constitutes today about 25% of our urban population. The newcomers from the rural areas amount to almost 15% of our total population. No statistics are really reliable in this field but a good estimate establishes that this population that we are talking about comes to between 20 and 30 million Latin Americans. Thus examples of that cultural imbalance we are talking about are readily apparent in each of the cities one visits in Latin America.

Everybody knows that Latin America is a continent of social extremes of the very rich and the very poor. It is a continent dedicated within the world economy's division of labor to agriculture and mining. Being located therefore within the primary sector of the economy it is necessarily handicapped by a very rigid class system. The mass of its people are caught within this primary sector by being engaged in agriculture and mining. There is a very thin secondary sector engaged in industrialization. Finally there is a rather bulky tertiary sector engaged in occupations which the economist calls services.

Now, since Latin America is suffering because of poor terms of trade, it's quite normal that the rate of capitalization, the acquisition of new money for growth, is lacking. Therefore the rate of industrialization is also too low.

CITIES THAT LACK JOBS And this is the point we wish to make: since the rate of industrialization is too low, the cities cannot absorb the rural population which is trying to invade them. Far more people move into the cities than can be given jobs. The rate of urbanization is much higher than the rate of industrialization. Thus our middle class in Latin America not only is weak but most of the time parasitical, coming originally from the farms and mines and having to jump over those who hold jobs in industry because places in this category are too few to be available to them. The only way to land somewhere is to penetrate the tertiary sector, namely, to get a post in government or in the services.

Thus we can understand what is happening to Latin America in the field of urbanization and what is happening to the people at the lower levels of life in Latin America as they attempt to better themselves. So far, few are succeeding.

TOO MANY FARMERS AND MINERS This same phenomenon we are describing can be described from a third point of view; let's call it the social-psychological approach. The farmers and miners of the primary sector cannot hope to get very wealthy for one simple reason. Raw material today no longer has the importance it had in the past because that primary sector is overpopulated and the worker caught within it has only, because of lack of skill, a very low rate of productivity. So that worker is necessarily poor. But that worker caught within the primary sector, whether it be agricultural or mining, is subjected to very strong influences through the mass communication media and by observation of the outside groups exploiting primary production within Latin America.

Because of these experiences the masses for the first time are really becoming aware not only of their needs but of the misery which their poverty creates. Their condition awakens in them new wants and what has been called a real revolution of aspiration. Suffering from an acute awareness that they cannot get out of their ghettos and that they are caught within a system which cannot fulfill their aspirations, revolutionary reactions are stirred up in these people throughout all of Latin America. Since the whole population within Latin America is aroused today to the possibilities of new regimes and new systems, it is necessary to say that Marxism receives important attention among these workers.

ROADBLOCKS TO DEVELOPMENT   Let's take a fourth range of consequences of what we have been describing up to now, this time from the point of view of the cultural and anthropological. As long as the Indio of the Bolivian Altiplano or the Venezuelan concado or the Chilean inquilino was confronted only with the rather elementary problems of his rural subsistence economy, his very poor skill and his very low education did not create immediate problems. But now because of technological advances within the urban belt or within some mining industries the requisites of development are being felt more clearly every day. And at least the intellectuals in Latin America are becoming aware of a lack of balance between what they are and what they earn. They are acquiring new sets of values, ideas, opinions, prejudices, on the one hand, and a new body of requisites for today's living on the other.

The Latin American of today is awakening to the fact that in this psychology, in this culture, there are lags and even roadblocks to development. He is becoming aware of the fact that, for instance, mass production which is today a requisite of economic development asks for planning, programming, saving, and that all of these factors are at least incompatible to some extent with the complete lack of sense for measurement of time and duration which often characterizes his milieu. In the past the Latin fit easily into a "mañana" habit and was never characterized by punctuality. This can be charming, but in the field of mass production it is deadly.

Here again the Latin feels that he gets caught in a dichotomy. He is willing to adopt a civilization where his attitudes and his behavior and his ideas and his opinions are in accordance with the requisites of development. But in the field of culture, to use the German terminology, he is not at all willing to give up his sense of life and to sacrifice it to the madness of work.

STRONG STATE, WEAK SOCIETY   To end this brief review of the highlights of the social crisis in Latin America, let's consider a final point. Let's call it the social-political approach. Latin American countries are characterized by the dichotomic structure of an all powerful, all present state, on the one hand, and the dust of atomized, unorganized masses on the other without intermediate organizations.

We have pointed out, for instance, the weakness of the labor movement. We could point out other lags within the social political structure of the Latin countries, as for instance the problems of strong centralization in administration or more simplified procedure before getting to the top of state organization. If we have an artificially large tertiary sector of the economy centralized in the hands of the few members of the so-called elite or the middle class of the parasitical type, it's quite obvious that the trend is going to be towards a centralized system. The politicalization of every sector of human life is typical of Latin American countries since the power is almost exclusively in the hands of the professional politician.

DANGERS FROM FRUSTRATION   That's why my fear for the

future of Latin America would be that the pressure of frustration would continue to grow. Some sort of demographic reordering may be required, because when population growth is as much as 5% in some central American countries, the problem is almost impossible. We need economic development, social change, cultural imitation. We need political restructuring. Marxism has presented itself as being the only promoter of those several processes which Latin America needs to overcome the burdens of its underdevelopment. Some people now believe that Marxist ideology is gradually losing its impetus or is at least becoming fragmented. In any case, Marxism is not as much of a danger as it was ten years ago. There is growing danger of the establishment of left of center military technocracies. Since our Latin American populations are so badly skilled and trained, there is the danger that the people really trained to carry out development are going to try to do it by themselves, using enough coercion, enough force, to go ahead even if they cannot achieve it by mobilization of the human resources available.

This may be the real danger for Latin America today, a kind you could call creole naturism, a new brand of Latin American naturism. It could be the more harmful because it's moving in some countries toward left of center. In such a case the only alternative would be a radical cultural mutation of the Latin American man in order to get him ready for mobilization into a new social system which, coming from the grass roots, including intermediate elements and finally embracing society at the top would be able to assure the economic development which would overcome the grave handicaps to which I made reference at the beginning of this paper.

SECTION II

Political Considerations

CHAPTER 3

The Phenomenon of Dictatorship

Renato Poblete, S.J.

The world thinks it knows Latin America through its record of dictatorships and frequent revolutions. The picture that results is a caricature of Latin America although it is based on some degree of truth. For a century and more political instability has characterized many of our countries. Mexico had 70 changes of government between 1810 and 1876. In the Dominican Republic 22 dictators rose and fell between 1893 and 1916. Paraguay was ruled by three dictators during the past century. Bolivia has known a hundred years of successive dictators and revolutions. From 1925 to 1947 Ecuador had 27 presidents. Betancourt in Venezuela was the first democratically elected president in his nation to finish his term of office.

The topic we propose to analyze is vast and complex. We shall not attempt an exhaustive historical review of dictatorships in the Latin American countries but will examine the problem from the viewpoint of the political, social and economic elements which are precipitating factors.

DISTINCTIONS AMONG COUNTRIES To speak of "Latin America" presupposes the reservation that one keep in mind the necessity of making clear distinctions between one country and another since each has its own pronouncedly individual characteristics. In the matter of dictatorships we again must make these distinctions.

In order to orient the problem of dictatorship, one must present it within the framework of the politico-social characteristics of the continent. Foremost among these is political instability. But this instability is only a symptom of a more radical problem—a lack of development of the various sectors of society. The political entity is stable when it is solidly integrated and related to the totality of the life of the nation. Political instability does not occur when there is a balance of rival political forces but when there is a lack of balance between the sphere of politics and the other spheres of life in society.

I suppose it could be said that France prior to De Gaulle —even in the midst of continuous changes of government— was more stable than some of our Latin American countries. The instability of these countries is not based on continuous changes of government but upon a lack of balance, of equilibrium, between the political sphere and other sectors of society.

In the United States and in Europe, politics is well balanced with other social systems. In Latin America, politics is a mammoth, pervasive force, always to be found in the army, among the students, in the economic world, in the labor unions. Everything in Latin America has its deep relation to politics.

POLITICAL HYPERTROPHY   It is important to keep in mind this hypertrophy of politics, this exaggerated compression within politics of all the elements that belong to the other sectors of social life. Everything is expected from politics, and politicians are blamed for all the evils the nation suffers. From politics is expected a continuous miracle of provision and problem-solving and politics in consequence has assumed the role of greatest importance in the life of the nation.

In conjunction with this we find a paradoxical situation among many of the people of Latin America—a lack of political consciousness in the sense of feeling that they belong to a national unity. When masses of the people are living in the margin of cultural, economic and political life, it is very simple then for the caudillo—the charismatic leader—to exercise an autocratic influence over them. The more primitive the group, the more absolute is the dictator's power. In such a society there are no other social structures capable of balancing the power of the despotic political structure. And this is both the background and the continuing product of all dictatorships.

In a well-structured society, politics should have a subsidiary role among the constitutive activities of the social body. In Latin America, sooner or later all activities end in politics since other intermediary structures have not been developed. The man who engages in scientific research has to use a good part of his time in securing and retaining political sympathy and help to enable him to do his research. It is not that he is politically-minded or has a passion for political maneuvering but simply that scientific research is not integrated with the industrial and economic systems, which could more properly provide the help he needs.

Another example of this dependency on the political establishment is the trade unions, of themselves relatively powerless and so compelled to enter into alliance with politics. Moreover, they depend to a great extent upon international trade unions, some of which are politically oriented.

Whatever it is that you want to do in Latin America, you have to be connected with politics. Thus the individual remains at the mercy of one sole instrumentality, the State.

Progress is difficult, not to say impossible, so long as there are no intermediate structures in the social mechanism. Political hypertrophy is not the monopoly of Latin Americans. It will result in any country that fails to develop these intermediary groups.

COLONISTS NORTH, SOUTH There are other causes of instability in Latin America. Some have said in the past that it is an inheritance from Spain. They feel that the years of Spanish authoritarianism rendered the colonies incapable of integrating themselves into a more balanced social system.

Because they had previously lacked independent *creole* authority, the colonies were unprepared to accept a more democratic authority.

In his book *Between Freedom and Fear,* German Arciniegas draws a comparison between the English and Spanish governments in the Americas. In the north, the colonists came in search of freedom. In the end, the founding of the North American colonies was only the obvious culmination of a process already begun. It was the reaffirmation of customs already ingrained in the social milieu. It was an evolution, not a real revolution, for these settlers were accustomed to autonomy. The authority of their governors was more democratic since they worked closely with the popular assemblies. From the beginning, the keenest concern of the North American colonist was for freedom of worship, and their hostility to the Church of England was evident.

On the contrary, Latin America was part of an empire. The Spaniards came to dominate and evangelize. The viceroy represented the king, who was an absolute monarch. The role of assembly in Latin America was secondary and represented extremely limited power. Independence in the Latin American nations entailed a real revolution since from the beginning they were forced to look for new political and social forms. Religious liberty did not exist in the Latin American colonies since all were obliged to membership in the Catholic Church.

UNASSIMILATED INDIGENOUS GROUPS This comparison will help in understanding the Latin American problem though it will not fully explain it. We must acknowledge that the political phenomenon has a direct correlation with demographic problems, such as the existence of large unassimilated indigenous groups as well as masses of mestizos, underdeveloped and deprived, who can scarcely be said to participate in twentieth century civilization. Although these groups form a part of the nation, they are not integrated either socially, culturally, economically or politically.

Despite the over-all demographic explosion, in some areas there exists the problem of low density of population with a lack of internal communication. In many cases there is even a language barrier.

The problem of an underdeveloped economy has also been a factor in forming Latin American social structure.

On the social level, the elements I have mentioned favor an internal lack of class structure that involves a juxtaposition rather than a social organization and integration. Democracy, on the other hand, presupposes a large scale integration of the people in the political-economic-social life of the nation. The masses of illiterates in Latin America who do not participate in these areas have no interest in government, though their interest and loyalty may be enlisted by the demagogue.

FORMATION OF DICTATORSHIPS   A dictatorship takes form when one or more pressure groups, unchallenged, seizes the power of government. In order to better understand the types of dictatorship found in Latin America, let us examine the different forms of revolution and the various ways in which the pressure groups bring their influence to bear.

Kalman Silvert distinguishes these types in his book *Reaction and Revolution in Latin America,* which is written in English. Silvert shows the relationship between dictatorships and the extreme individualism found in these countries.

The first type of revolution named is what Silvert calls the simple barracks revolt. Most of the outbreaks, especially in the past century, have been of this kind. The barracks revolt occurs typically in a big class society. It is carried out by the army, sometimes in its own name and sometimes in behalf of a chosen leader. This type of revolution rarely causes widespread public disturbance since it represents merely a switch in government from one general to another.

The second type, the peasant revolt, is generally of little significance and limited in effect to a locality, though the Mexican revolution at the beginning of this century would perhaps fall in this category.

Third is the regional revolt, common in the early days of Latin American independence. Here the caudillo strove to put down provincial revolts and to centralize power in an authoritarian regional government. Typical of the caudillos who led regional revolts was Rosas of Argentina.

The fourth, a more modern type of revolution, Silvert calls the complicated barracks revolt. This is an insurrection that involves civilian as well as military groups, with widespread military action. The issues are ideological and relate to political parties as well as other interest groups. The Cuban revolution in its beginnings might be considered an example. Although this is the most prevalent type among modern-day revolutions, exceptions are the revolts which overthrew Peron in Argentina, Perez-Jimenez in Venezuela and Rojas Pinilla in Colombia.

OTHER FORMS OF REVOLUTION   Still another type of revolution, the civilian-political revolt, is no longer an important consideration since modern armies are capable of swiftly dispersing such outbreaks. However trade unions on general strike bear some resemblance to this type.

Social revolution is the next type described. A social revolution is one that implies a change of social structures. The Mexican revolution in 1910 and 1917 is an example. The Peron revolution in Argentina and the Bolivian revolution of 1952, led by Paz Estenssoro, might also be considered in this group.

Since 1945, ten countries have had still another type of revolution, called the community barracks revolt. These are Guatemala, El Salvador, Honduras, Puerto Rico, Panama, Venezuela, Colombia, Ecuador, Brazil and Bolivia.

When Arciniegas wrote Between Freedom and Fear in 1952, most of the Latin American countries were under governments which were the products of some type of revolution and most of these were dictatorships. In a few countries (Paraguay, Haiti, Nicaragua and the Dominican Republic),

barracks revolts were still very common. Three countries—
Mexico, Uruguay and Chile—were under stable democratic
regimes.

Two important facts should be mentioned here. First, that
even the countries that have experienced a democratic regime have had some revolutions. There were a number in
Mexico, for example, during the first fifty years of this century. Secondly, we would like to point out that many revolutions have been in a certain sense counter-revolutions to
put down dictatorships.

Some revolutions are proper to a big class system, as is the
barracks revolt. Others are characteristic of areas in which
the middle class is growing and seek an adjustment. In countries with a well developed sense of nationality, the revolt
is of a more complicated type.

This variety of Latin American revolutions that we have
described does not imply a continuous change of government. Latin America has had a series of extremely long dictatorships, among them Gaspar Rodriguez de Francia, who
controlled Paraguay from 1814 to 1840, and his successor,
Carlos Lopez, who was in power for 20 years. In Venezuela,
Antonio Guzman Blanco was in power from 1870 to 1888
and after a lapse of years we find the dictatorship of Juan
Vicente Gomez from 1908 to 1935. Santo Domingo was controlled by only three men during the last century.

CAN DICTATORSHIPS BE PREVENTED?   What are the elements
of this pattern of political development in Latin America?
How can we prevent the phenomenon of dictatorships?
Why did some countries give rise to a series of dictatorships
while others did not?

Immediately following independence, all the Latin American countries fell to one degree or another into a lengthy
period of disturbance, the causes of which were varied. One
important element of political unrest during this early period
was what is called *caciquism*. The *cacique* would be a man
who had fought in the wars for independence, but his deter-

mination to retain and increase his power as a local leader proved disruptive in the struggle to gain national cohesion and strength.

The period of the caciques was followed by one in which revolutions prepared the way for dictatorships, each based on a personality of great popular appeal and influence. The caudillos of this period achieved political unity for their countries.

Silvert points out in his book that all the Latin American countries have had a dictator as a factor of integration. Diaz in Mexico, Rosas in Argentina, and Portales in Chile—these men are to Latin America what Louis XIV was to France, Ivan the Terrible to Russia, Bismarck to Germany. Unification by rule of the strong man seemed an indispensable step in attaining national unity and a strong centralized government. The same has been true of European countries.

TRANSITION TO THE NATIONAL STATE   Following the periods of caciquism and caudillismo came that of transition to the national state. This may be described as a point in evolution when a nation reaches the process of institutionalization, that is to say, when the role and the status of the president are well defined, when we know what is expected from the man who happens to be president, when the office of president is more important than the men who are in it, when it is the office and not the personality that counts.

Some countries of Latin America have not yet evolved beyond the stage of caciquism. It would appear that some of the countries of Central America have had too many caciques and have not been able to unite them. It is probable that Argentina would now be made up of numerous small nations had it not been for the powerful dictatorship of Rosas, who forcibly united the caciques.

It is difficult for many countries to make the transition to the national state since demographically, economically and socially they are more regions than nations. Here life is informal, the frame of reference is the local, and there is no regional integration. Thus there may be such a multiplicity of groups and of leaders that no one individual can control the country.

It is not easy to arrive at a national consciousness, especially when a country has the difficulties previously mentioned—the problems of class structure, of an underdeveloped economy, of low density of population and lack of communication.

Countries that have not evolved beyond caciquism may normally be expected to pass through a series of revolutions and dictatorships. Caciques and caudillos tend to be dictators. Their use of force will produce an action and reaction of forces.

In general, we may say that countries which have experienced the unifying action of the caudillo have been freer from revolution. Chile, since Portales, has had an extremely orderly constitutional life. The genius of Portales was to institutionalize the country. Before the ideas and exigencies of the nation, his role as caudillo receded. His wish was not to remain as a charismatic leader but to transfer the symbols of leadership to the nation, so that the focus of the concept of civic dignity and power might pass from personality to guardianship of the general interest of society. He was able to instil a true national image in place of the caudillistic reverence and fear. This explains why Chile has been unique in its advancement toward national consciousness and unity.

THE ROLE OF INTERMEDIARY GROUPS Dictatorships appear where intermediary societal structures are lacking. These intermediate groups act to cushion the tensions between the individual and the state.

When society is well balanced, the pressure groups are well balanced—economic groups, trade unions, student groups, churches, the military, and so forth. But when any of these groups becomes excessively powerful, we face a sort of dictatorship from a group or from a person within a group. An example of this kind of power seizure is the rise of Peron, backed by the powerful trade union movement in Argentina, a country with a very large middle class.

It is evident that caciques and caudillos must rely on the use of force and must therefore have at their disposal some agency that will provide it. The first pressure group that we shall consider is the armed forces.

Edwin Lewin in his book *Arms and Politics* distinguished the different roles of the army in Latin America. First, we have what is called the para-political role. Here the army prepares the way for the government, supplements and jealously guards its action. It purports to guarantee the stability of a country hovering between revolution and return to constitutional normality. During this time between overthrow of the dictator and the return to constitutional government, the country needs strong hands to maintain stability. This function of the armed forces is quite common in countries where popular revolutions have ended caudillismo. Venezuela after the downfall of Perez Jimenez was a case in point. The army took over the government in the interim before elections. The same thing happened in Colombia and Brazil.

The army also can prevent the ascendancy of one particular group, as it did in Argentina. After Peron fell, the army was in control during the transition to Frondizi's government.

INFLUENCE OF THE ARMY   Intervention of the army may be brief, but it always presents a danger. The pledge to relinquish power once normality has been restored may be slow of fulfillment since experience has shown that it takes time for the army to realize that constitutional government has indeed been re-established. The army claims that the country will be prepared for democracy when there are evidences of perfect order, discipline and uninterrupted work, all of which are circumstances difficult to find. So the hold on power is prolonged. The army thinks of itself as the source of order and the protector of individual rights. It will remain in power as long as it sees fit.

The second role of the army is demonstrated in countries

where there is a more or less stable constitutional life. The army has a purely political function of veto. That is to say, it has allowed the governments to work within their constitutional limits but imposes its own policies upon them. So long as the government acts within the limits fixed by the army, it has liberty. An example of this: A few years ago the army in Argentina exercised its power of veto on the policy of Frondizi, actually deciding his policy on relations with Cuba.

The third role of the army is purely professional, as is the case in Chile and Uruguay. The army in these countries has a specifically military role relating to the national defense, though they also play a subsidiary role in integrating the peoples of their countries through adult education and technical assistance programs.

Unfortunately the army has often over-played the first role described—the para-political—and too often in collaboration with the oligarchy.

It may be asked whether it is necessary or advisable to maintain such well equipped armies in Latin America. An indication of the view of the United States Government may be found in its expenditures on military aid to the Latin American nations, although for many years there have been no wars in Latin America.

THE ROLE OF THE CHURCH The second pressure group to consider with regard to dictatorships—let us be very frank—is the Catholic Church. We know that the Church, or more precisely, the ecclesiastical authority, has played an important role in Latin America. The influence of Christianity as a set of ideas and values must be distinguished from that of the structural Church with its own proper authority. We shall deal only with this last aspect, not with the ideological aspect of the Church.

The Catholic Church has always tried to maintain good relations with all types of government since it has continually sought a structure for fostering Catholic education, the avoidance of propagation of error, and the teaching of

Christian morality to the populace.

The influence of the Church in Latin America varies widely from one country to another. In some countries the Church and the state are still united by concordats, in others they are not. In some countries the influence of the Church is diminishing under the impact of secularization. Pluralism with regard to doctrines and morals places the various ideologies more or less on the same level. So the ideology of the Church no longer carries the weight that it has in the past.

In those countries where caciquism and caudillism still prevail, the ecclesiastical authority has given a limited importance to the legality of their status and has looked with some benignity on the caudillos and dictators, showing friendliness provided they do not attack the Church but leave her free to teach morals and doctrine. In general, the Latin American Church has not been preoccupied with safeguarding individual liberties as are Christians now in the communist states. The consideration of the Latin American Church was undoubtedly the common good. The lesser evil was chosen; since the dictator had full power, it was thought to be more prudent not to antagonize him.

THE CHURCH AND THE DICTATOR   Dictators know well that in some ways they need the cooperation of the Church. This is very important. It leads them to give aid to Catholic education, and to be quite severe in a negative type of morality, while they ignore completely that most important element of morality, an appreciation of human liberty.

In many cases the beginning of the end of totalitarian regimes has been a fight against the Church, as was the case in Argentina, Colombia and Venezuela. But also in many cases the beginning of dictatorships had a sort of blessing from the Church. During the struggle for independence, the Church was identified with the making of the nations. Since that time it has not been entirely separated from political events. During the last century its position regarding the dictators was dubious. Carrera in Guatemala, Garcia Moreno in Ecuador, were the Church's children of prediliction. In this century the picture has changed, although Laureano Gomez and Peron were very closely related to the Church and backed by its authority as defenders of Christian principles.

In short, the ecclesiastical authority has frequently given an excessive importance to the privilege of Christian religion and not enough consideration to the excesses of some dictators. A concept of the role of the Church that relegates it strictly to the teaching of Catholic morals and doctrine has given rise to the notion that the Church should never interfere in politics. This has resulted in undelayed acceptance by the Church of the totalitarian regimes that have risen in the more developed countries.

OTHER SUPPORTS FOR DICTATORS   Among the pressure groups, students are also important, especially in relation to ideological movements. Student groups are sometimes related to dictatorships in a negative way by reason of the fact that the overthrowing of the dictator was due to a struggle begun by these groups in the university. In some other cases they have fought against democracy—for example, the extreme leftists in Caracas who agitated against Betancourt.

Another pressure group is the oligarchy, which has been closely involved with dictatorships especially in countries with a big class society. Using the army as their instrument, they have plotted to retain control of the nation and to put an end to social reform. Most dictators have been too closely tied to the oligarchy to be inclined to foster moves toward social betterment. But with the growth of the middle class and the increasing power and organization of the trade union movement, we may predict that totalitarian regimes based on the power of one family or that of an oligarchical group will be less and less in evidence.

Finally, there are pressures from foreign business concerns and from foreign governments. The name of the United

Fruit Company calls to mind a long period of exploitation under powerful totalitarian regimes in Central America. Foreign companies have looked upon such dictators as Trujillo, Rojas Pinilla and Batista as guardians of economic stability, who enable them to quietly carry on their prosperous concerns.

THE UNITED STATES AND DICTATORS   To what extent has the United States Government aided the rise of dictators in Central and South American countries? The case of intervention in Nicaragua, and the relation between the National Guard and Anastacio Somoza, are worth consideration. It would probably be difficult to prove in what measure the Pentagon has had part in establishing dictatorships or overthrowing governments. Although imperialism is no longer an issue, still the influence of the United States is very strong.

The Germans and the English have also wielded powerful influence in some South American countries and have been very much involved with some of the dictators.

Some Latin American countries have had interests of great importance in neighboring countries. Peron exercised enormous influence in revolutions in some other countries and upon their subsequently established dictators.

In order to understand why foreign governments and businesses have sometimes favored dictators, one can begin with the simplest of explanations: affairs are expedited if you deal with one man. You don't have to wait until things are approved by a congress. To a foreign country operating in Latin America, it is of primary importance to have a stable government—stable at least in the sense that business can be carried on safely, with no disruptions.

The full limits of responsibility for Latin America's dictatorships cannot be determined without consideration of the foreign policies of some European countries and of the United States over the past century. What can be said, for example, of the United States intervention in the Dominican Republic from 1916 to 1934? Was the purpose the defense

of oppressed people and their liberties? Was it to defend the
people or to protect American interests? Historians so far
are divided on the question.

WERE DICTATORS NECESSARY? Given the circumstances of
the Latin American colonies at the time of liberation, are
dictatorships necessary? One can only point to the incidence
of the phenomenon in Latin America. A study of the history of the Latin American nations should give considerable
knowledge of what may be expected in the emerging nations
of Africa and Asia. Already they have shown a marked par-
allelism to the development of nations in Latin America.

Latin America's hope of a more balanced and stable political organization lies in the integration of the masses and
a balanced development of social structures. A necessary
enabling factor is economic development. Once we have
achieved these things we may hope, not only for integration
within countries, but for integration of all the Latin American
countries so that the continent will become a land of peace,
progress and understanding.

CHAPTER 4

Christian Democracy and Social Reality

Rafael Caldera

It would not be just to say that until Fidel Castro seized power in Cuba nobody in the United States or in Europe cared about the future of the nations of Latin America. But it is not an exaggeration to admit that only after the establishment of an avowedly marxist-leninist government on that beautiful Caribbean island, major efforts have been initiated to study and understand the serious problems posed by our social reality; to analyze and interpret the difficulties over which our political organization has stumbled; to formulate plans for cooperation, rooted in that international solidarity by virtue of which we are entitled to ask a revision of systems and a readjustment of relations in search of a universal common good.

Twenty politically sovereign entities, almost all of them liberated through heroic efforts at the beginning of the nineteenth century, have been struggling more than a century for the achievement of political stability and the solid establishment of an efficient democratic system. On February 15, 1819, Liberator Simon Bolivar, addressing the legislators gathered at the Congress of Angostura which was to give birth to Great Colombia, pointed out the need to seek a government capable of achieving "the greatest possible happiness, the greatest possible social security and the greatest possible political stability." The objective, by his own definition, was not purely of a political nature or, even less, ideo-

CHRISTIAN DEMOCRACY AND SOCIAL REALITY 55

logical. Eight years later, in a letter addressed to Bolivar, his fellow countryman Andres Bello, the greatest Latin American scholar, the centennial of whose death will be commemorated next October 15, observed that "the stability of institutions in circumstances such as ours does not depend so much on their intrinsic goodness as on extrinsic supports, such as those lent by the personal qualities of the individuals who administer them." He added that, with the wounds of recent war still open, the first objective was "to establish public order on foundations which, inspiring confidence, will make our devastated fields, our commerce and our revenues to flourish anew."

THE BURDEN OF WEAK ECONOMIES   What a hard task it was, indeed, at a time when the world was overrun by the most unfettered individualism, and the Latin American republics, fiercely attached to their political independence, still lacked the essential economic foundations to set in motion their own development! Organized with parallel economies, there had been no interchange among them nor was there any stimulus toward such. As long as they depended on a decadent colonial empire, the metropolis was the natural center for intercommunications and their market for the raw materials that were their only means of subsistence. Their separation from the empire was attained through the wars of independence, but other industrialized or rapidly developing nations simply moved in to replace the ancient metropolis. Through commercial treaties, we were kept chained to the production of raw materials, thus assuring the industrial nations of permanent sources for their own development and progress.

When the wars of independence ended, the new republics were overwhelmed by debts contracted to finance the pursuit of liberty. The history of these loans is fraught with pain for the nations of Latin America and with shame for the capitalist countries who brazenly exercised the ignoble art of usury. The effects of these debts on our precarious fiscal structure, on our feeble administrative morality, on our political stability and even on our formal sovereignty were felt in many nations of our continent well into the present century.

At the same time Iberoamerican man, once charged with his own responsibility, confronted a task of a magnitude completely disproportionate to his scant resources.

VAST UNCOLONIZED AREAS   The territory remained largely to be colonized. Even today, almost every one of the nations of Latin America has great extensions of land still uncolonized. In the case of my country, Venezuela, almost half of our territory is practically uninhabited; in some sister republics the proportion is even greater. While the coastal regions of the Atlantic, the Pacific, the Caribbean and the Gulf of Mexico are densely populated, still the heart of the continent is virtually unexplored and beckons to the spirit of adventure offering an incalculable reserve of hope. Yet there are those who believe and declare, in the face of our demographic explosion, that the remedy is to limit the population instead of undertaking with courage the task of placing the world at the service of man; there are those, as Paul VI has noted, who wish to remedy the scarcity of bread on the table, not by adding more bread, but by trying to seat fewer people at the table.

Those immense territories, with abrupt impassable mountains and torrential rivers, offered almost insurmountable barriers before technology introduced the bulldozer and the jeep. These lands were also in the thrall of endemic tropical diseases. Malaria issued a constant warning to man that he should not dare to penetrate them. The anopheles mosquito jealously guarded the heartland for the future generations. If we had mines, we lacked the capital and the technology to exploit them by ourselves. If the fruitful land produced large crops, their processing always remained out of our reach. Meanwhile the oscillations of the market in the great industrial centers—fluctuating in response to the sacrosanct law of supply and demand—led to commotions in our fragile

economies that were even greater than the convulsive trem-
ors resulting from political ambitions and usurpations of
power.

UNCOMPLETED RACIAL FUSION At the same time, Latin
American man was experiencing in the nineteenth century
the culmination of a process of racial fusion that had begun
three centuries earlier. It is to the credit of the Spanish and
Portuguese that they did not allow the three great ethnic
elements that made up our population to stagnate into dis-
parate segments. But it fell to the new republics to complete
this process. It was they who, overcoming great internal
difficulties, abolished the ignominy of slavery. But they did
not stop there: the aboriginal Indian, the former African,
and especially the man of mixed blood who, in some places
such as Venezuela, by 1800 made up half of the population
—conquered, through war and at the price of many other
sacrifices, the fullness of equality.

The achievement in actual fact, and in the spheres of
power, of an effective equal participation, regardless of what
pompous constitutional texts might proclaim, did not come
in many areas except through violence.

The drama endured by Latin Americans in their search
for a new social organization within a framework of democratic institutions has been regarded sometimes with contempt, not seldom with acerbity and almost always with
injustice. The emergence of Africa into the world scene,
populated by those who, until only yesterday, were deprived
of all rights; their tormented efforts, despite the fact that in
general they were not forced to endure a long and cruel
war of emancipation as in Latin America, may give at least
an approximate idea of the obstacles that we confronted in
our lands to organize the new republics. This, in spite of the
fact that, as Bolívar remarked, "we were already old in the
usages of civil society." We had universities before they existed in North America; we had minorities who were well
aware of cultural developments in Europe, though perhaps

less up to date in the advances of technology; but we also
had inherited from the colonial structure huge illiterate
majorities who, in many cases, not only did not know how
to read and write, but had not received the most rudimen-
tary instruction for earning a decent living.

WE UNDERSTAND TODAY THROUGH YESTERDAY   It is necessary
to understand all the real elements of the Latin American
drama to visualize the magnitude of the problems and of
the undertaking that must be faced by the men of this generation. Moreover, the very links of solidarity that today
tighten world relations have served to make even the hum-
blest human being aware of the fundamental idea of the
rights of the human person. To him these ideas are embodied
not only in the theory of free expression of thought and of
participation through suffrage in the organization of public
power, but also in more concrete form in the right to eat a
full meal, to live under a decent roof, to found a family, to
receive an education, to have amusement and leisure and to
participate in the essential comforts that civilization is making accessible to all.

And this very psychological intercommunication, through
the press, radio, television and all other media of mass communication, plus the incessant efforts of commercial and industrial propaganda to create new necessities and increase
the number of consumers, have taught our peoples to aspire
rightfully—and sometimes to the detriment of their economic structures—to all these achievements, such as the
refrigerator and the air conditioner, the radio and television
sets, the automobile, which all make up the image of a
modern welfare civilization.

AFTER WORLD WAR I   The aftermath of the first World War
was not without its effect on the mentality of a new Latin
American generation. An effect limited, perhaps, to the upper strata, and especially to the intellectuals. Except for
the very peculiar phenomenon of the Mexican revolution

and some other equally unsuccessful movements in other countries, these times were not marked by great upheavals of the masses. However, in the circles of the intelligentsia and especially in university milieus, the ideological crisis suffered by Europe had considerable repercussions.

The prevalent worldwide unrest, the skepticism that shook the more cultured peoples, the loss of faith in a democracy that had only led to totalitarian outbursts, the effervescence of communism and of fascism, the bankruptcy of traditional values: all this was bound to leave its mark on the thoughts and behavior of the generation that began to act during the third decade of the twentieth century. The anguish of the reality they faced led them easily toward the Marxist ideology that was beginning to be applied—before the astonished eyes of the world and to the surprise of idiots through the audacity of Lenin.

It is true that in some countries—those that had enjoyed a more stable political life, such as Chile, Colombia or Uruguay—the old party structures still persisted. But the struggle between Liberals and Conservatives, once meaningful in the context of the emerging republics, was losing its meaning unless it was sustained by the personal magnetism of its leaders. Against those old political structures a new ideology was rising, cradled in the universities and high schools, in literature and the press, and in the embryonic labor unions. In countries such as Venezuela, oppressed throughout the first third of the century by an iron dictatorship that swept away the old parties and kept us isolated from the world in which we lived, the coming of freedom was a clarion call for the new ideas. Old politicians, full of merit, called upon their people to rebuild the ancient party organizations, but not even the halo of their sufferings as victims of the tyranny moved the people to structures that they regarded definitely as a thing of the past. A similar story might be told of the Dominican Republic, when in 1961 it unburdened itself after 30 years of oppressive dictatorship. With certain variations due to differences in time, it will be told of Paraguay or Nica-

ragua when the teams that currently govern disappear and
the people can breathe deeply of the air of liberty.

AFTER WORLD WAR II   After World War II the impact of the
great world currents on Latin America was even stronger.
They were divergent and complex currents, but all centered
around ideas that hammered at the conscience of man: social justice, better distribution of income, the dignity of the
human person, the economy at the service of man, access of
the people to political and economic power, struggle against
colonialism and imperialism; in a word, the struggle for the
attainment of sovereignty, not only in the political field,
but in the cultural and economic spheres as well.

All these ideas, surging in confusion through the conscience of modern man, struck a chord of deep pain and
anguish when confronted with the realities of Latin America.

We Latin Americans realize that it is time to fulfill the
destiny of our peoples; but at the same time we are aware of
the fearful obstacles that our social reality places in the path
of this formidable task.

It is no longer a matter of maintaining cultural elites, but
of incorporating into the process of development all the segments of our population.

Reality is beginning to be studied through scientific analysis and interpretation. Statistics abound, and, as they are
repeated they increase anguish, the anguish of time, the
anguish of conscience, the suffering of a still unconquered
destiny.

For a population exceeding two hundred million, the time
passes and can only be regarded with optimism in the measure that makes noticeable the magnitude of the problems
faced and helps to understand the urgent need to plan and
execute a profound change of structures.

ELOQUENT STATISTICS   In rough terms, of every two Latin
American families, one inhabits a dwelling that does not
meet the minimum requirements of comfort, hygiene and

human decency. The report of the experts for the meetings at Punta del Este in 1961 pointed out that the housing deficit was growing by more than one million units each year. Of every two children of school age, one is entirely deprived of any chance to attend school, and a high percentage—it has been estimated as high as 90%—do not complete their primary education. In 1960, according to the New York Times' figures, per capita annual income in Latin America was estimated between $300 and $350, as compared with $2,400 in the United States. But of our twenty countries, only five attained or surpassed this average; the other fifteen fell below it. In Bolivia and Haiti, the shocking figure was less than $100 per person per year. If we analyze the distribution among the various social strata we reach truly horrifying figures.

I have mentioned only some of the outstanding items which shock the conscience of Latin American leaders. Going from effect to cause we find that they are rooted in the very structure of our economies, and a little research uncovers facts that exasperate man's innate sense of justice.

PRODIGIOUS ECONOMIC HANDICAPS   More than a century after independence we continue to be providers of raw materials. The international markets, dominated by the industrial nations, have often experienced annual price fluctuations between 10%-20%, with a tendency to decline or at least remain static. Meanwhile there has been a sustained increase in the prices of manufactured products, thus resulting in a progressive deterioration for the Latin American economies, of the international terms of trade. As it has been observed, a consequence has been that in fifteen years the value of goods exported by the United States to Latin America has tripled, while the value of raw materials exported by Latin America to the United States has not even doubled.

A consideration of these facts is essential to an understanding of the political mentality that prevails on our continent. The course of events cannot be left to the gradual development of natural forces, especially when these are often influenced by the selfish interests of monopolies or oligopolies, rather than by the general interest.

Yet the social process advances dynamically. Half our population is under eighteen years of age. Meanwhile the process of industrialization and the progress of technology demand an even greater investment of capital while offering employment to a proportionately smaller number of persons. Thus the unemployment index rises and oscillates between 10 and 14%.

Only revolutionary change can alter the trend of these figures and set a new course for the future. We accept the rejection of the term revolution when used as a synonym of violence and unrestrained impulse to change everything. We acknowledge the observations which, based on the above definition, were expressed by Pope Pius XII in his Pentecost message of 1943, and Pope John XXIII in his encyclical *Pacem in Terris.* But to uncounted Latin Americans who defend institutions while demanding structural changes, as was once lucidly pointed out by Hubert Humphrey, now Vice-President of the United States, the word revolution carries the sense of a change that is neither gradual nor spontaneous, as mere evolution supposes, but rapid, deep and at the same time guided by new programs and ideas.

IMMINENCE OF REVOLUTION   Thus we affirm that the imminence of a revolution is palpable. Either we carry out a peaceful, constructive and Christian revolution, or our peoples will be dragged to their own misfortune, into a violent, materialistic and destructive one. The circumstances I have described, and the influx of ideological factors, explains clearly the development of the different political forces existing in Latin America. Exact sketches cannot be traced for all the different countries, but despite their diversity there exists a fundamental unity.

On the one hand we find the traditional forces that competed in the old parties: Conservative and Liberal. In some countries they still subsist with identical or similar denomination. In Colombia—by virtue of a constitutional reform approved through plebiscite when a military dictatorship was overthrown—they have assured themselves the distribution of all positions of power for a period of sixteen years, of which only six have elapsed. However, the anachronism of this system became strikingly evident during the last elections, when the proportion of abstentions reached 70%; that is, only 30% of the electorate was inspired to vote. In other countries, such as Chile, Conservatives and Liberals still display strong organizations, but the number of votes they receive has declined substantially. Their differences, as we know, had centered mainly on ideological and political matters: their attitude toward religious questions was often the dividing element; Liberalism entered the political scene waving a banner of a militant secularism.

NEW POLITICAL STANDARDS   In some places Liberalism perhaps also represented the emergence of an urban class dedicated to commerce, banking, transportation and in general to the circulation of goods; and connected to foreign capitalism while Conservatism was more representative of the landlord—often latifundist—class. Another party that appeared in some countries within this historic framework was the Radical Party, sometimes led by the incipient industrial bourgeoisie, others by the middle class. It was not entirely alien to the old quarrel between clericalism and anticlericalism. In general, as happened also in France and other European nations, it was simply an addition to the old picture of Conservatism and Liberalism, sometimes even forming fronts within them for the defense of order and democracy, fronts which were often at the same time opposed to programs and movements inspired in social change.

MANIFESTATIONS OF MARXISM   Against an impenetrable Right, which has resisted the transformation that social structures demand, marxism has proliferated and spread in a variety of manifestations. Born of a common doctrinary basis, differences have arisen among the orthodox groups adhering to marxism-leninism: they have occasionally been subject to deep cleavages, such as that currently opposing the followers of Moscow's line and those oriented toward Chinese aggressiveness or Castroite communism or existentialism. It should be noted that both currents were originally bred on the theory that they would achieve power only through violence, and establish a dictatorship of the proletariat as a transitory step toward a Socialist society.

Today, however, it is not only the marxist-leninists who find their roots in marxism. Many former communists, or dillettante marxists, have drifted toward different positions. They are grouped today, together with non-marxist persons who yet desire a change of system, under the common denomination of democratic socialism. This name has been given, in international meetings, to the youth of such varied parties as APRA of Peru, Accion Democratica of Venezuela, Colombia's Liberal Party, Paraguay's Liberal Party, Chile's Radicals, Argentina's Frondizi Radicals, the Popular Party of Puerto Rico and the Liberation Party of Costa Rica. In its very variety lies its main problem. These parties have filled a great role and at a given moment commanded the allegiance of popular majorities in several Latin American countries. They have counted among their leaders men of undisputed prestige. But their lack of clear definitions and the inconsistency between a revolutionary doctrine full of marxist terminology and a pragmatic and often incoherent line of action, has led to a rapid deterioration of those forces. Their greatest weakness lies in the continuing decline of their emotional appeal to youth.

SYSTEMS OF FORCE Another frequent feature of Latin American life has been the military dictatorship. The acuteness of existing problems, the incompatibility among the various currents of opinion, the loss of prestige of the popular systems, has often led to the eruption of a system of force. In a few cases, as recently in Bolivia, it has received popular support. Explanations and justifications have abounded, but almost invariably these movements resulted in personal or group hegemonies, self-perpetuated until the inevitable violent overthrow. We have often heard comments on the incapacity of the Latin American people to achieve a democratic life, but our best thinkers have explained how, rather than being the result of ineptitude, this phenomenon derived from such factors as the aftermath of the wars of emancipation, with its legacy of civil wars and their byproducts, the strengthening of caudillos, the resulting crisis in moral and political values, and social and economic difficulties. On more than one occasion political anarchy has opened a wide door to usurpation. Frequently military coups have been a reaction to revolutionary regimes insincerely led and inefficiently managed. But in the long run ambition reveals itself, and governments based on force, clashing always with the rebelliousness of the people, end without solving any important problems.

It should be noted that in addition to the right-wing dictatorships, military regimes based on left-wing programs have also been attempted. There is much current talk of "Nasserism," although in Latin America the only major experience of this type has been under Peronism. But experience has shown that dictatorship can never achieve a development compatible with the dignity and the demands of the human being. The increased civic maturity of the people and the growing institutional conscience of the armed forces are positive factors that help to allay the inclination to adventurous coups.

RISE OF CHRISTIAN DEMOCRACY   It is within this framework that a new political movement has recently appeared: that of Christian Democracy. Marked as the only growing democratic political force in Latin America today, it is now recognized—after having been often ignored—as a vigorously emerging force of the future. I believe that the above background summary will help to understand it and to better appraise what it represents for Latin America.

The Christian Democratic movement of Latin America achieved its greatest repercussion yet through the brilliant victory of Eduardo Frei Montalva in the Chilean elections. Actually this event had been preceded by certain important milestones. In the Chilean municipal elections of May, 1963, the Christian Democratic Party displaced the Radical Party, which traditionally had held first place among political organizations. In July of the same year, after the support of the Christian Democratic party gave the victory in the Peruvian elections to Fernando Belaunde Terry, the Christian Democrats became part of the new government, and in December their candidate for Mayor of Lima, Luis Bedoya Reyes, decisively defeated Sra. Maria Delgado de Odria, candidate of an incredible coalition: that formed by APRA and by the followers of ex-Dictator General Manuel Odria.

In the elections of December 1st, 1963, Venezuela's Christian Democratic COPEI Party—originally named Committee for Independent Political Electoral Organization—obtained 22% of the votes, gaining second place in the electoral results and revealing itself as the only party that had grown since the previous elections. To both national and foreign observers this fact marked it as the favorite in the next electoral process, if its growth should continue at the same pace.* A few days later, the young Christian Democratic Party of El Salvador gained second place in the congressional elections, obtaining fourteen of fifty-two seats and winning as well the mayorality of San Salvador and several other towns.

CONTINENTAL GAINS OF A NEW IDEA   In addition to these noteworthy milestones, many additional symptoms could be observed: the growth of the party in Brazil, especially in the

---

* Doctor Rafael Caldera, the author of this article, was the COPEI candidate for president in the contest in which the party registered these notable gains.—Editor's Note.

states of Sao Paulo and Parana; its sudden appearance, with tangible results, on the political scene of Bolivia; its consolidation, through the adoption of a system of proportional representation, in the Argentine elections; its attainment of third place in the Dominican Republic elections that chose President Bosch, and of fourth place in the Panamanian elections of 1964—in both these cases it was recognized as the first of the small parties and the one with the greatest growth potential. We should note too, its presence and its combative vigor, under adverse circumstances, in Guatemala and Colombia, and its incipient but promising existence in almost all the other nations of the continent. One should not forget its signal role in Uruguay, where as the oldest Christian Democratic Party of Latin America it helped point the way to the party in all the other countries.

ROLE OF UNIVERSITY STUDENTS Thirty years ago, many of the present leaders of Christian Democratic parties were only university students, bent on the study of the social encyclicals and of the Catholic Action programs. They soon understood that political activity is an essential aspect of social action; that it is necessary to separate politics from religion; that politics demands the presence of men capable of working for ideals, with honesty and devotion, especially in countries as needy of clear guidance as are ours, due to their painful past experience; and that the political field can prove to be one of the most fruitful for the generous activity of those who enter it to fulfill a duty of service.

These young men began thus to enter the political scene, caught always between two fronts: struggling, on the one hand, against the selfishness of the indifferent, of insensitive capitalists, of those attached to tradition for tradition's sake and opposed to the changes demanded by justice and the social reality. On the other hand, they confronted materialism, totalitarian marxism, with its false promises inspired in hate, and in contempt for liberty and the dignity of the human person.

The struggle was difficult and complex. In some countries it was necessary to face oppressive dictatorships, risking not only loss of liberty through prison or exile, but personal and family safety as well. In other cases, powerful organizations controlled all means of mass communication and distorted our positions before public opinion, when they did not silence them altogether. It was necessary on more than one occasion to endure irreverence and slander, and it took a tenacious effort to pierce the curtain of silence that prevented our words and our ideas from reaching the people.

SUPPOSED CONFESSIONALISM   Christian Democracy has had to overcome many misconceptions. One that is still prevalent is its supposed confessionalism. Christian Democracy is not in any way a religious movement; nor does it have a confessional character. Christian Democratic parties include among their members Catholics, Protestants, Jews, agnostics, professing the widest variety of conceptions and creeds. The name Christian does not represent a religious position but the conviction that Christian values and the spirit of Christianity can best fulfill successfully the requirements of social justice and defeat marxism in the struggle to conquer the soul of the people. We believe that the Social Christian inspiration overflows the boundaries of a given creed. And it is pleasant for us to observe how the ecumenical spirit developed in the Second Vatican Council has come to reinforce the attempts at rapprochement among all men who understand and support democracy, who share the principle of social solidarity and defend the imperative demands of social justice.

You will not be surprised by now when I say that the position of Christian Democratic movement is definitely revolutionary. We do not defend tradition for tradition's sake. We accept from it what represents essential values or is part of the spiritual heritage of our peoples; but we are profoundly convinced of the need for change, and that this change must not be gradual or superficial. We defend property, but we demand that it fulfills a social function. We stimulate private initiative, as long as it is not incompatible with the collective welfare. We believe in friendship among peoples, especially those that defend the same fundamental values that inspire Western civilization, but we feel that this friendship cannot be based on dependency, privilege or imposition, but on a relationship of decorous equality. We maintain that by virtue of international social justice the wealthier and more developed countries are obliged to lend their support to those which, due to various circumstances—not always or entirely within their control—are not in a condition to achieve by themselves, in this highly interdependent modern world, the goals they have set themselves.

A NEW CONTINENTAL POLITICAL FORCE The growth of Christian Democracy has modified considerably the political horizon of Latin America. Only yesterday, observers saw nothing but the communist threat, a dictatorship to oppose it, or the so-called popular parties, as a temporary and declining barrier to the communist avalanche. This panorama has changed. The youth in the universities of Latin America is becoming decidedly enthusiastic about Christian Democratic formulas. The disquieting stream of marxism in Latin America's educational institutions is beginning to lose ground. We could name many countries where Christian Democracy is a thrusting force in this field. Not only in Chile, where the movement is already in the government, nor in Venezuela, where it has achieved a front rank position, but also in countries where Christian Democracy is still an incipient force, as in Colombia or Bolivia. Youth gets behind coherent ideologies that offer complete solutions to the problems with which it is concerned. Communism is one of these coherent systems, seeking to interpret all the phenomena of the cosmos, from the origin of matter to the final destiny of man; Christian Democracy is the only other system that is able to offer a similar cohesion, with the advantage that it nurtures in the spirit of youth, its faith in absolute values, and makes it feel that not everything ends with death or has its only expression in material terms.

SOCIAL PROJECTION OF CHRISTIAN DEMOCRACY   But what interests us above all is the social projection of Christian Democracy. The social problems of Latin America are extremely grave. They cannot be resolved simply by the injection of a few million dollars: as statistics show, this is less than what we lose through decreases in the prices of our products. A more fundamental change is needed, and this must be clearly understood by the other countries of the free world, especially those to which we are related, such as the United States. The people of Latin America desire a revolutionary change. They want it because they need it. It is senseless to wait any longer. It is naive to prepare formulas that operate slowly, in the long run.

Circumstances are so serious, that there are those who, in good faith and even with the support of authoritative currents of Christian theology, come to preach and maintain the need for violence. In opposition to this, the Christian Democratic thesis calls for a peaceful revolution, a revolution in freedom. We understand the arguments put forth by what we might call the "theology of violence": we are profoundly convinced that violence only engenders further violence and that while it hastens the destructive state of revolutions—that is, the destruction of the old order that is deemed unjust—it obstructs, and sometimes renders unfeasible, the constructive state, that is, the establishment of a new and just order. Christian Demoracy is, therefore, firmly opposed to violence.

In the pulsating situation of Latin America, a victory of Christian Democracy appears more and more each day as the only encouraging alternative. This does not involve the exclusion of other social-political forces, including Democratic Socialism, which still has a role to fulfill. But the initiative, the sense of direction and responsibility demanded by the change to be accomplished are so great, that they require an ideological cohesion and a tactical sincerity now found only in Christian Democracy.

The people had begun to understand this, even before the wire services deigned to acknowledge our existence and began to honor us with their attention, recognizing our true nature without cliches and distortions.

COMMUNISM, MENACING REALITY Communism in Latin America is a menacing reality. It becomes more threatening each day, encouraged by the failure of the incomplete solutions and the inconsistent attitudes of Democratic Socialism; it is nourished by the injustice perpetuated through the static postures of the Conservative—or Liberal, or Radical—right; stimulated by the regimes of force, since each dictatorship leaves behind it a wider perspective and a more aggressive organization of the militant communist ranks, ready to command and twist the spirit of the people in its struggle to recover liberty.

This threat is also fed by the psychological stimulus derived from marxism-leninism in other regions of the world: the stability of the so-called "people's democracies," even if they are maintained by force through the most oppressive police system; the strengthening of China as an aggressive world power; the disturbing news from Viet Nam; the anguish of the entire Asian Southeast and the open help received by the Congo Reds and other communist groups in Africa. But, most of all, by the brazen activities of Cuba, training guerrillas, distributing all types of propaganda and sending material help by sea and air in its determination to convert the whole of Latin America into a great guerrilla camp.

The Right is powerless against this danger. A perfect example is found in the former government of Chile, where a government coalition of Conservatives, Liberals and Radicals, under the leadership of one of the most competent men of the private sector, left behind it a situation in which the extreme Left obtained 40% of the vote, in the midst of a dizzy inflationary process that rocketed the prices of basic commodities, obliterated the modest income of the working forces, especially the peasants, and turned to quicksand the ground on which the new administrators must rebuild the economy.

RECORD OF DEMOCRATIC SOCIALISM   As for Democratic Socialism, its experience in government has generally been characterized by a lack of clear aims and of ambitious solutions. Its internal disintegration is grave. We need only to observe in Peru the profound disillusionment among the people due to the entente between a group such as APRA and the followers of Odria, who once persecuted them, and who repesent a rigid conservative position. Similar examples can be found in other countries and the resulting mass exodus of followers has led in two directions: toward communism or toward Christian Democracy. In Venezuela this trend is expecially noteworthy, since the traditional majority party which won 70% of the popular vote in 1947, fell to 48% in 1958 and 33% in 1963.

LATIN AMERICAN INTEGRATION   To complete this landscape, we should add that Christian Democracy has raised one of the most beautiful banners that currently excite the imagination of our peoples: that of Latin American integration. We shall cease to be small, poor and relegated countries as soon as we unite and act as a single force, made up of twenty sovereign nations but linked in a single idea, expressed with a single voice. Integration presupposes a state of mind; it demands mutual trust; it requires decision and firmness. The achievement of these requisites goes hand in hand with the growing influence of the Christian Democratic parties. Not in vain have we joined in an organization that has already celebrated six regional congresses, the Christian Democratic Organization of America (ODCA), over which I have the honor to preside, and whose favorite topic has been precisely that of the political, economic and social integration of Latin

America. This organization, together with that of the European Christian Democratic parties (NEI) and of the Christian Democrats in exile from the Iron Curtain countries (Christian Democratic Union of Central Europe), make up the World Union of Christian Democrats (UMDEC), which has already held four congresses. It fosters interchange among the parties of Europe and America, which naturally differ due to the disparity of circumstances between industrial and emerging nations, but nevertheless are more closely united each day in their fundamental conception of the destiny of man. In addition, they are currently developing coordinated programs for leadership training.

A PHENOMENON BORN OF SOCIAL REALITY In Latin America then, the Christian Democratic parties constitute a phenomenon born of the very social reality in which they act. I wish to insist on this, or I would risk a misunderstanding. We are based on a doctrinary conception, but the application of this doctrine is adapted to the requirements of Latin America's social condition. Our disagreement with the traditional Right, our attitude toward regimes of force, our struggle with the marxist-leninist Left, our differences with Democratic Socialism, result from the inability of all those forces to resolve the problems afflicting our peoples.

It has taken North Americans and Europeans a long time to understand us. Sometimes they have dabbled in the internal politics of our countries, alternately supporting dictatorial regimes, right-wing governments or the populist parties. I once pointed out to the late President Kennedy the danger of maintaining extremely close links with a given political force. Our peoples are still highly sensitive about colonialism. The encyclical *Mater et Magistra* noted this and remarked that wealthy countries giving aid to the emerging nations must be very careful to respect their personality, which derives from the habitat, from ancestral traditions, from natural disposition; that they should take care not to influence for their own profit the politics of these countries, in a spirit of domination, for this "would be, it must be stated frankly, a new form of colonialism, which although disguised under a respectable name would in no way differ from the domination that many countries have only recently overcome."

"PERHAPS THE ONLY HOPE" In its sincerity, in the clarity of its words, in the firmness of its conduct, Christian Democracy constitutes today the best, and perhaps the only hope for the people of Latin America.

Its growing popular support is the most encouraging sign in our continent. And the destiny of Latin America is a key factor for the security of this hemisphere and for the health and progress of Christian civilization. Our peoples have heard much about agrarian reform, industrialization, structural reforms, social security, fight against unemployment, education, housing, sanitation, culture and welfare accessible to all. The road, however, seems long; it demands great courage, great energy and decision. Christian Democracy, among the various ideological and political forces of Latin America, is the best qualified to travel this road. It seems that from now on, she will fulfill this extraordinary task.

CHAPTER 5

Communists and Other Marxists

Rev. Héctor Samperio G.

The representatives of communism in Latin America today are a minority but an impressive one—dynamic, well organized, well trained and equipped. They are for the most part dedicated to their subversive ideology. An estimated quarter of a million are party members. There are many more followers who are not party members.

Beginning in 1918, communism in Latin America was directed by the Soviet Union. Later Chinese communism arrived. Castroism is the new form of marxism to become popular. In every country the links of communication trace through the embassies of these communist governments and through direct orders from the Red Bloc.

In order to operate in Latin America, even marxism, which aims toward a society without classes, must depend upon the power and potential of the existing classes. Communists in Latin America are workers, peasants, students. They come from the lower, middle, and upper middle classes. Some are professionals—artists, journalists, teachers and politicians. Of special importance are the middle classes, from which communism has regularly drawn its best leaders, either in terms of organizers, agitators—those who move the masses and propose issues to arouse the interest of the masses—or propagandists, who provide the answers on the issues and the basic doctrine to the masses.

In the strategy of international marxism for establishment of the marxist order, infiltration and domination of the political system is the primary aim. But in Latin America other objectives are considered important: first, infiltration and eventual control of the workers' unions and peasant organizations in order to quicken the class struggle that will result in economic chaos and thereby facilitate seizure of power. Professionals and politicians are important to this effort. Second, they aim to make the best possible use of transitional periods needed to move from a capitalistic society to socialism and finally to communism. Third, to suppress or render ineffective any resistance, whether from native structures such as the Church or from a foreign country. Fourth, to infiltrate and control the social communications media and increase marxist propaganda.

Other strategies are used by the communists in Latin America but these four are the most important. Tactics employed to implement these strategic moves are varied according to national and international circumstances. The approach to the workers and peasants is almost always the first step.

BIRTH OF THE PARTY IN LATIN AMERICA Following the Russian Revolution of 1917 and the establishment of the Communist International, the party was introduced in Latin America by a membership drawn from Brazilian anarchists, Mexican revolutionaries and socialists in Uruguay and Chile. During World War II the peak was reached both in party membership and in communist influence among the workers. At that time there were some 150,000 more party members than there are today and the Latin American Confederation of Labor, known as CETAL, flourished.

Since the war, open communist unions or confederations have been organized wherever possible. The most recent continental effort in this line was the creation in 1962 of a center for Latin American workers with headquarters in Chile. In addition they seek to infiltrate the existing unions. They look for the man with leadership potential. They then train him and help him obtain the top offices in his union, after which they can direct or influence the unions' policies.

This tactic of infiltration is widespread in Latin America but perhaps most common in Bolivia and Mexico, in spite of the fact that most unions in these countries are affiliated with the anti-communist ORIT, the Inter-American regional labor organization.

The peasant classes have been neglected until recent years, the only exception being the Mexican *Ligas de Comunidades Agrarias* back in the early thirties. Rural communist groups have since appeared in Brazil, Peru, Chile, Colombia and Mexico. Their main tactics have been invasion of the latifundias, with experiments in a kind of socialism and, as in the case of Colombia, the use of violence.

PENETRATION VIA THE STUDENTS   Among the students similar tactics have been used quite openly. With a potential force of some 500,000 people in Latin America, the students are a prime target. Among them are some actual party members and a large group of marxist followers. The university student, idealistic and generally unprepared by insight or experience for realistic analysis of social problems, is ready prey to the easy solutions and rousing slogans offered by the communists. The students are easily incited to action.

Alberto Campos, a communist at San Marcos University in Lima, Peru, told a group of students in 1962: "Peru has many problems. We must have an agrarian reform. We must nationalize our industries. I am only working with students now, but in a few months I will go to the mountains to educate the peasants. They do not yet have a revolutionary consciousness. I will give them that."

He made good his pledge. Together with Hugo Blanco he was responsible for the Indian uprisings around Cuzco. The demands of the Indians were, of course, quite just, as has been remarked many times. But the Cuzco revolt serves as an example of how the communists use demagoguery to capitalize on the real needs of the people and to promote their own aims and goals.

Professionals and politicians are prized communist recruits.

Philosophers, artists and writers, such as the Brazilian architect Oscar Niemeyer, the Chilean poet, Pablo Neruda, and the Mexican painters, Diego Rivera, Clemente Orozco and Alfaro Siqueiros, have given considerable prestige to the communist cause. For obvious reasons, teachers are regarded by the party as especially valuable. Infiltration of the teachers is perhaps the greatest single communist threat in Latin America.

SPECIALISTS IN PROPAGANDA   Of great importance also are the journalists, for they mold public opinion. Communist printed propaganda continues to proliferate despite the large financial deficits involved. A popular Mexican magazine, well known in many Latin American countries, reportedly suffers a yearly loss of $600,000. Another bi-monthly magazine operates at a loss of $170,000 per year. There are at least 25 communist or pro-communist publications in Mexico alone and in addition to a multiplicity of publications made available by Russia, Red China, Cuba and other countries behind the Iron Curtain.

The huge propaganda apparatus which troubles us in Latin America is not limited to the press or even to radio and television. It includes movies, the drama and—least expensive but effective—the fence covered with chalked or painted slogans.

Again for obvious reasons, the infiltration of top governmental offices is another primary aim. Guatemala in 1957 and Brazil in 1964 are the most dramatic examples. In addition to increasing the potentiality for seizure of power, such infiltration makes it possible to support in various ways the foreign policies of Cuba and the Soviet Union.

COMMUNISTS AND THE MIDDLE CLASS   The communists have no ideological objection to recruiting the upper middle class though its income is derived from private professional practice or from investments. They are not regarded as capitalists. The distinction lies in the fact that they are not connected with national or foreign capitalistic enterprises or monopolies. Actually the main target of the communists is not the lowest classes but the middle and upper middle classes, where more potential leaders will normally be found.

Very important to the communist struggle to prevail over opposing forces is the propaganda apparatus which employs the various communications media as well as public demonstrations. By these and other means they secure support for the foreign policies of countries whose governments they have infiltrated.

The internal Latin American structure that the communists aim to suppress is the Catholic Church. In this they are proceeding with great caution. Chinese communist experts have worked out in detail the plan by which the Church is to be overcome. The advance should be made "two steps forward and one step back," say the planners. Propaganda should be made to exploit the historical issues which give the Church the appearance of a negative institution insofar as the freedom and social development of the people are concerned. First the Catholic social organizations, and later those that are religion-oriented, must be infiltrated. The Church must continually be represented as a foreign power, allied to the capitalistic world. The communists will unflaggingly harass her, exploiting her human mistakes and weaknesses. They will fight the foreign clergy and confine the influence of the Church to her own internal structure and the private Catholic home. By capturing the mind of the youth in childhood, they can afford to leave the adults alone. Through these and other means they will make the Church a thing of the past.

This plan of the Chinese communists is being carefully applied throughout all Latin America. The drive against the Church was recently reinforced. In 1963 the Church was designated as the primary goal in Latin America by the ideological commission of the Communist Party.

A serious setback to the campaign against the Church has been Catholic social leadership in some Latin American countries—the renewal of the Church and the awakening of an active, social-minded Catholic laity.

AGAINST THE YANKEE IMPERIALISTS Resistance to the anti-communist influence of the United States in Latin America has been fomented and inflamed by communist propaganda against the Yankee imperialists. They promote among the people a violent nationalism, exploiting the historical issues of U.S. intervention in Latin American countries during the past century. They represent the U.S. socio-economic aid program as directed only toward the protection of the national interests of the United States by maintaining the Latin American countries in a status of dependency. They back the foreign policies of the Soviet Union and bitterly criticize those of the United States.

Since the Cuban Revolution, emphasis has been on the following tactics, varied according to local conditions: (1) terrorism through serious guerrilla warfare in the backland, a weapon generally used when other tactics have failed. It has been extensively used in Venezuela and is a threat in Peru and other countries. (2) Creation of popular national liberation fronts to enlist more people, to agitate and push the election of communists—also to back the foreign policies of Cuba and the Soviet Union. (3) An increase of propaganda and infiltration of power centers—unions, universities, governments—to gain support for policies of disarmament, non-intervention and self-determination.

The popular front is founded as an organization with a large leftist membership entirely controlled by communists. It is a mass movement which can be characterized as anti-imperialist and pseudo-democratic. Thus the communists contrive to operate through parallel organizations involving leftists who do not ordinarily wish to become communists. Since 1961 this tactic has been effectively used in several Latin American countries.

Despite serious setbacks in Brazil, Chile and Bolivia, and a decrease of influence in Venezuela, communism is still very much alive in Latin America, looking for revenge in Chile and threatening good relations between Brazil and Uruguay, where most of the Brazilian communists fled. The communists are busy increasing their flood of propaganda, discrediting democratic institutions, offering technical assistance to those who will lead rebellions, and fostering the deterioration of national currencies to precipitate the economic chaos in which they can proceed to a quick and easy seizure of power.

THE POTENTIAL OF COMMUNISM What seems to be the potential of communism in Latin America? Thus far we have seen something of the kinds of people who support or actually belong to the Communist Party, and how they are achieving their objectives. It is also very important to analyze and evaluate their prospects for success or failure.

Within the context of the theme of this conference, The Church and Social Revolution, communism offers an alternative answer to the problem. One must not become so exclusively concerned with communist activities as to forget that the movement is based on an ideology to which many communists are sincerely committed. In the present situation the critical question is the extent to which a strictly materialistic ideology that promises a society of equality and justice will appeal to the impoverished masses of Latin America.

Let us briefly review the factors in favor of communism and those against. Douglas Hyde and other experts have cited the following as contributing to the progress of communism: first, bad social conditions—malnutrition, destitution, poor housing, illiteracy, bad or inadequate education. These factors are of equal importance to the communist movement. But I would stress this: The people in Latin America who have little or no education—the peasants, for example—do not distinguish between the economic proposals of communism and those of a more balanced ideology. The communist proposals look fine to them, and they are neither aware of nor concerned about the consequences of the system involved. Few know what communism really is. One of our chief concerns should be to instruct our people so that they know what communism means.

Secondly, extremes of wealth and poverty existing side by side, and an absence of social conscience on the part of the wealthy, have given rise to a widespread determination to bring about social change. The more this change is opposed by the ruling group, the stronger the determination of the people becomes. The situation is not improved by the fact that often those who work for justified and needed change are labelled as communists by those who oppose it.

OTHER FAVORING FACTORS   A third factor that favors communism is the growth of materialism since World War II. Our resistance to marxism has been weakened by a loss of spiritual values, a hedonistic attitude toward life on the part of our youth and adults, and the disintegration of family ties. Even if communism should disappear from the scene, this growth of materialism is a sufficiently great calamity to our society.

Fourth and fifth factors aiding communism are the inadequacy of our present social structures in face of a population explosion and the political instability which in many countries invites communist take-over.

Finally, Latin American communism would receive an enormous boost if Castro, with the aid of other Red nations, succeeds in making Cuba an economically advanced and prosperous country. Cuba would then be a living demonstration to the other countries that the communist socioeconomic system does succeed.

Now for conditions that are unfavorable to marxism. First, economists are not supermen but sometimes fail as well as succeed. They are subject to divisions among themselves and they do make mistakes. Latin America is still a testing ground for international communism. Tactics and strategies are under continual modification. This necessity to experiment might eventually work in their favor if, in their continual testing of strategies, they are coming nearer to the appropriate ones.

The Alliance for Progress, though it had a dubious start, now seems on its way to substantial accomplishment in the relief of Latin America's social and economic problems and may thereby provide a considerable force against communism.

THE ROLE OF THE CHURCH In the socio-economic field the Church has taken the lead in agrarian reform and social development in many of our countries. Examples in Chile, Brazil, Peru, Bolivia and other countries are very well known. In spite of handicaps, the Church has made impressive strides forward. Basic education programs, cooperatives, credit unions and other social assistance projects are now widespread throughout the continent. There is, of course, a need for more. New dioceses, more and better seminaries, are needed in order to secure adequate spiritual and social assistance for our people.

As it strives toward renewal in Latin America, the Church keeps clearly in mind the goals for mankind delineated by Pope John XXIII in his last encyclical, *Pacem in Terris*— truth, justice, charity and freedom. These four principles alone can provide a secure basis for our society.

The important fact about the Latin American Church is not that it lacks money and personnel to carry out the programs it envisions but that it has undergone a true *aggiornamento*. The first reform to make is by all means that of the Church itself. The encyclicals of Pope John and Pope Paul and the work of the Vatican Council are the providential means of renewal. The Church all over Latin America is committed to adapt the eternal message of good tidings to mankind within its milieu—to our Latin American people of this time and of the times to come.

The liturgy is transforming the spirituality of the people of God. Pastoral programs under the direction of the hierarchy are reaching the people as never before. New techniques of the apostolate are renewing Christian action. And, very important, an emerging laity, more conscious of its role within the Church and in relation to the modern world, is taking the avant garde posts in the task of transforming the face of Latin America into one which will reflect the truth and justice of the message of God over the message of a materialism that enslaves the people.

SECTION III

Socio-economic Considerations

CHAPTER 6

Christian Social Movements in Latin America

Marina Bandeira

Mexico in years past went through a bloody revolution. Cuba is a warning to us all. But Chile has shown us that bloodshed is not inevitable in this struggle for integral development.

Is it possible to release the whole of Latin America from underdevelopment? This is the great challenge which must be placed before the Christian social movements in Latin America.

The most significant features, the ones to which I would like to call the attention of the social movements, would be:

1) the acceleration of history;
2) a tendency towards communitary living;
3) overall planning;
4) the emergence of a third, underdeveloped world;
5) the increasing cosmopolitanism of man, or the new planetarian man.

1) *The acceleration of history.* As from the beginning of the 19th Century, the world has witnessed the speeding up of progress through technical expertise. The Industrial Revolution created new societies, new comforts, through ever improving techniques, through social, economical and scientific methods.

All this brought a new type of chain reaction throughout the world; modern man hopes that all may benefit by a yet greater acceleration in scientific discovery; he is no longer fatalist, and he will not wait for any so-called normal process of evolution to bring his grandchildren some nameless benefit in a far distant future. Instinctively, he assumes his proper role of man as subject of culture, subject of history.

2) *Tendency towards communitary living.* This rapidly changing world is reacting against the individualism of the past centuries. Social groups with local, national and even international loyalties are drawing together in a more organic unit.

Social experiments are being undertaken all over the world. Some aspects of life in capitalist countries such as boards of directors for the sharing of responsibility (the socialization of decisions) prove this tendency.

The interdependence of interests, be it in labor unions or employers' associations, are indicating the new possibilities of negotiating solutions by social groups within a country, negotiating solutions between countries or even groups of countries.

Brute force, all-powerful persons, organizations, or countries, have more difficulty imposing their will.

More and more the tendency is to discover new social articulations of groups, of social units, of political regimes which are able to recognize and accept this interdependence that has been discovered.

On an international level, this concept finds its most typical expression in the admission of the principle of coexistence.

3) *Overall planning.* If governments are to meet the demands of their people, they can no longer afford to be empirical, shortsighted or simply idealistic. Governments are required to organize the march of progress, to make plans for the solution of problems, to establish priorities in the execution of these plans. Governments are becoming more powerful and more is expected of their capacity for organization. Sociology, statistics, public opinion polls, and the possibilities of making a scientific analysis of facts, all allow for the reduction of risk; but the measure of responsibility and power

which thereby falls to governments is proportionately increasing. If, during the last century, the Industrial Revolution had the characteristic of harnessing physical force, today the phenomenon of rationalization, especially through planning, allows the decision-makers to reach the organization of social life itself.

4) *The emergence of the third world.* The contrast between fully developed and underdeveloped countries is another characteristic of our times.

It must be recalled at this point that this same problem, this same contrast exists within countries. In my own country, Brazil, we find areas of extremely fast development which are becoming richer every year while the typically underdeveloped areas, the majority of the country, are becoming poorer and protesting against this state of affairs.

The Second World War and the years that followed it saw the great awakening of the "backward" peoples. The poorer countries began to accuse the richer ones of being responsible for their distress and castigated all colonial exploitation. This new type of nationalism declares that underdevelopment is not an inexorable decree of fate. The poorer countries demand fair prices for their products.

The meeting of African and Asian countries at Bandung in 1955 should not be ignored. The meeting at Geneva, in 1964, of the Conference of the United Nations Trade and Development, showed Latin America closing ranks with other underdeveloped continents. It is the third world coming into existence. The third world is not necessarily against the rest of the world. Together they want to find solutions for their common ailings and fight for the enforcement of decisions which will benefit them all.

5) *The planetarian man.* More and more, man feels himself to be a world-citizen. The problems of Indonesia, Tanganyika and Cuba can influence his life directly, and he is beginning to realize this. At the same time the inhabitant of Indonesia, Tanganyika or Cuba, is discovering that he can influence the destinies of the whole world. The populations

of even the poorest countries demand that their own interests be respected and consulted. They are beginning to sense that a true "internationalism" can only be born if it rests upon true and healthy nationalism and that, therefore, internationalism embraces the interdependence of all nationalisms.

When science is allowing us to see the training of future interplanetary pilots, we begin to realize that we will not render good service on other planets if, before arriving there, we do not learn to understand and respect one another on this our own planet. Through a new form of cosmopolitanism, capable of respecting the different cultures and backgrounds of one another, a new type of attitude is beginning to appear in men who, without despising or relinquishing the culture of their own countries, are learning not to impose but to communicate with men who originate from different backgrounds, from other cultures, even if materially those countries have not yet put to use the latest technical resources.

These new men do exist and their number is multiplying. President Kennedy was one of them. They are sensible enough not to try and impose their solutions, their way of life on other countries because they know they might have successful immediate results but, in the long run, the artificial solutions would not last.

Are there other clear trends? Are the trends which we have mentioned wrong or incomplete? The important thing is to have in mind the main tendencies of the whole world, whatever they are, when we examine a detail of the world: Latin America. This is what we will try to do now: Whither goes Latin America?

LATIN AMERICA AS WE SEE IT   Latin America has embarked on a course of social, economic and political transformation and the clock cannot be set back.

Profiting by the lessons of other countries, there is a marked tendency in Latin America today towards discovering a new form of social organization that does not submit either to the materialism of the developed affluent countries of the West, or the massification of the Soviet bloc.

May one ask: are the efforts towards a Latin American self-expression valid? One thing is certain: new social structures will appear. Is it going to be a harmonious society reached through an integral development, with no encouragement for passive, frustrated herds? This question must be asked of the Christian social movements in Latin America. Their role is not static: theirs is not "to do and die" as the poet said; theirs is "to *reason* why" and fight desperately to open the way for man. Fight for a society that can be a living testimony to the basic duty of a Christian which is to love God and to help our neighbor come closer to the image of God, physically, intellectually, spiritually.

What, then, is preventing us from putting into practice the solutions which are desired by millions of Christians in Latin America at the present time? Is there a ready answer? Which are the clear alternatives placed before Latin America and, therefore, before the various Christian social movements in our continent?

THE ALTERNATIVES BEFORE LATIN AMERICA We are living in a rapidly distintegrating society and this intoxicating experience provokes shocks and tensions. This is a fact.

Although there are other interpretations of this fact, I adopt the view that the tensions between the different social groups in Latin America resolve themselves into two ideological groups, even if their views are unconsciously expressed or, in some instances, interweave themselves.

The first is the *ideology of conservatism,* of all those who are satisfied with the status quo, who point to administrative and political corruption and immorality as the root of all present evils. For those, the solution is more order and honesty—and the problems will solve themselves and all will live happily ever after.

Those who oppose this view say that the evil has deeper roots: the structure of their countries will have to be modified in order to obtain a fair share of development for all, a better distribution of wealth and new wealth that will benefit all. This is the *ideology of transformation,* or the ideology of reformism, or the ideology of the social revolution.

The bitter antagonism between these two fundamentally opposed positions has caused deep wounds on both sides and, most unfortunately, this antagonism is to be found among Catholics, among Christians.

These two ideologies, of conservatism and transformation, correspond to two main historical projects: the first one corresponds to the ideals of the beneficiaries of the European Industrial Revolution and its successful followers.

The ideology of transformation corresponds to the historical project of those who suffered the consequences of the unbridled prosperity of the others.

These definitions are not static. It is possible for conservative groups to evolve into transformist positions and viceversa. It is not true that a clash beween the two has been pre-determined by history. I am looking at them as they are *today.*

THE SPECIFIC PROJECTS   To the main historical projects we have referred to, conservation and transformation, there correspond various specific historical projects and their specific ideologies and philosophies.

This is where the problem becomes more involved: When the statement of generalities begins and the arguments become heated. Therefore, it should not be a loss of time to try to give the meaning which is being attributed here to the various specific historical projects to be chosen as alternatives by Latin America.

Headed by the ideology of conservatism, we will find its principal branches:

Capitalist liberalism: which, although dead and buried in its home country, England, still finds its followers in present day Latin America. These theories, in their absolute sense, are still accepted by Latin American capitalists and, what is more, by representatives of capitalism from other countries where these theories have been outlawed through antitrust legislations, income tax restrictions and other similar controls.

Neo-capitalism: refers to all social-economic systems which distribute increasing advantages to workers, to the extent of offering humane working conditions. But the last instance, the supreme decision, belongs to capital, to money, because money controls the means of production. Therefore, neo-capitalism is a new form of capitalism, a bland one, which accepts the existence of the rights of labor, but it is capitalism.

Let us content ourselves with these two specific projects with regard to conservatism. Our intention is definitely not to discourse on these subjects, it is simply to establish some starting points for discussion.

Now, with regard to the ideology of transformation, we would sort out:

Socialism: in broad terms, includes all economic systems which assign property and decisions to the State. This is the strict meaning of the word. Its extreme form is collectivist communism. The opposite trend will be found in the British Labour Party and calls itself democratic socialism. Another one is the socialism of Israel.

Marxism: Finds great acceptance among intellectuals in Latin America who wish to adopt the marxist principles but do not accept the Russian, or for that matter, the Chinese solutions. These marxists stand for nationalism and want to find, within the marxist doctrine, their national forms of self-expression.

Leninist-Communism: There is no risk of misinterpretation here. In Latin America, the Russian branches (which include Stalinist die-hards), the Chinese, the "trotskyists" and the nationalist marxist fight one another but, just the same, create dangerous problems in our continent. Yet a hysterical fear of communism can have no less disastrous consequences: namely, the unthinking species of anti-communism which confuses the legitimate aspirations of the people with communism itself. Such irrational fear spreads panic in the upper strata of society and only increases the tension between the wealthy and the poor. The misery of the people should be fought even if communism never existed.

Social Catholicism: in various forms and with different names has been sprouting in different parts of the world since the 1914 War and the Social Encyclicals. In France, the Social Weeks, the Catholic Action, the Christian Trade Unions have been grasping for a new form of social self-expression.

Most of these attempts have been greatly affected by a philosophy of Christian inspiration: personalism. The encyclical, *Quadragesimo Anno*, developed still further the ideas previously outlined with regard to social and individual use of property, fair salaries, intervention of the State when there is abuse by economic-powers. A special mention could be made of the influences of men like Theilhard de Chardin, Maritain, Mounier, Romano Guardini, Lubac, Congar. Together with other groups connected with Father Lebret of *"Economie et Humanisme"* there is a tendency towards a new form of social organization generally referred to as "Solidary Civilization" which would be the sum of countries organized in a personalist form of government pledged to promote integral development of the person within the community (local, regional and national).

To this must be added the influence of "active non-violence" groups inspired by the movement promoting Civil Rights in the United States, and various European organizations. These groups, who count many Catholics among them, are beginning to make their appearance in Latin America.

The Christian Democratic Parties in our countries are very diversified. Their quality varies as well. The present great risk and temptation of our Democratic Parties is the importation of ready made foreign models, and also, foreign money for national party politics. In some countries the antagonisms inside the parties are stifling them. But, just the same, the Christian Democratic Parties in some of our countries are definitely maturing and making headway.

Social Protestantism: Protestant denominations have been concerned about the same problems, also after the First World War, in England, Germany, France, the United States. Currently a professor of theology at the University of Princeton, Richard Shaull, who knows Latin America well is having his writings read with increasing interest by young Latins, including Catholics.

These are the conflicting ideologies, the conflicting historical projects we find in Latin America. They are there and cannot be ignored. We Christians must be present in this conflict, but, as I said before, our purposes must be very clear.

THE LABORERS FOR THE HARVEST   Who are the laborers who will have to find their way through this forest, this maze of conflicting ideas and harvest the wheat?

The Church which, more and more, wishes to serve and be poor, wants to estimate its potential to put it at the service of all. We must, then, make an appraisal of the possibilities we really represent in Latin America for the efforts in the social field. Who are the Catholics in Latin America?

Some years ago it was possible to classify lay Catholics in Latin America in three main categories: Nominal Catholics; Cultural and folk Catholics; Formal Catholics or "good Catholics."

This leads us to a new type of Catholic which is multiplying rapidly: the *committed Catholic.*

The committed Catholic, of his own free choice, wants to live the message of the Gospel, the doctrine of the Church to its ultimate consequences.

This attitude of the committed Catholics creates an antagonism with the formal Catholics of the upper classes who, very frequently, have adopted an ideology of conservatism and do not even understand the meaning of words like paternalism, "assistencialism," alienation, instruments for the perpetuation of capitalism, which are frequently thrown at them and which are answered with phrases like fellow travelers, dupes of Moscow, red Catholics, and similar expressions.

But these are the laborers for the harvest: the nominal, the cultural and folk Catholics, the formal and committed Catholics. These are the ones who have been chosen to give testimony of the message of Christ. The first Apostles were not very much better and did not quarrel much less. We must do our best, and the Lord will not forsake us.

TASK OF THE CHRISTIAN SOCIAL MOVEMENTS   Faced with all these challenges one realizes the prime importance of the Christian social movements in Latin America.

In the cultural field: The role of the Catholic schools and all types of educational organizations of all levels is decisive. Groups which, instead of developing personalities—intellectually, humanly and spiritually—are teaching passivity and cramming brains, are not working for Latin America. They are working to conserve the present situation.

We desperately need people who can create. We do not need to prepare people who can rubber-stamp the existing errors.

In the economic field: The Christian movements must have the courage to fortify their growing personalities. They cannot satisfy themselves by filling empty bellies temporarily, keeping man in a state of dependence. The efforts must lead to the creation of conditions for men to feed themselves and guarantee their security. They must foster the creation of ever more effective types of rural reform, of grassroot activities which should bring about economic independence; new forms of relationship between employers and employees where there is no room for robots.

If communication between human beings is love, the Christian social organizations and activities must be able to continuously look for new forms of expression of charity in the relations that result from intercommunication in society.

In the political field: Through direct education and the

activities of social groups, the Christian must help his fellow men acquire conditions to participate in the political process. Let us not keep the campesinos apart because they are illiterate, or find any other excuse. They are as human as you or I. We do not have the right to be "afraid" of the masses. We must communicate with the people, help the mass become people, each individual capable of acting by conscious decision.

The worst form of atheism is that of transforming our brothers into objects. Let us not forget that in its deepest sense, charity means helping, promoting the other human being.

The duty of Latin American Christian politicians, the representatives of the people, is to perpetuate creation through the improvement of new forms of communitary living based on fellowship, cooperation and service in which all can have their share in a harmonious society.

ORGANIZED SELF-EXPRESSION   At this point of discussing the possibilities of Latin American self-expression it would, perhaps, be worthwhile to recall that a new mentality of a "Latin American Continent" is growing in reaction to the old Pan American ideal. The new mentality does not necessarily mean antagonizing the United States. It stands for the need of leadership for an organized Latin America with clearly stated ideals and solutions and, therefore, in a better position to negotiate, to discuss with the materially powerful friends from the North.

An organized Latin America would be able to place on the table its views and discuss them, instead of making us witness the strengthening of undercurrents which breed hate and frustration and won't help any of us: from the North or from the South.

In the Catholic Church, the creation of CELAM, *Consejo Episcopal Latino-americano,* has played a decisive role which can only lead to a permanent improvement of understanding within the Church.

The strengthening of Latin American structures can only lead to efficiency, to avoid waste of energy and resources. These structures, which would be the sum of proper national organizations, through proper representation, could only lead to simplifying to a tremendous extent the mechanics of the relations within our continent and the friends who wish to help us but find themselves facing a vast continent with various different cultures, enormous economic differences and stages of development, presenting thousands of individual requests for funds, technical assistance and personnel.

We represent a problem, a headache, a puzzle, for those who wish to help us. Let us help them help us by organizing ourselves.

We have a gigantic effort before us, the integral development of Latin America. Let us establish an immediate operational target for ourselves: the dynamization of the legitimate, authentic Latin American organizations.

The proper Latin American expression in the social field, through its various branches would offer our friends from the United States in particular, and also other countries, the possibility of channelling all the assistance that is being given, in personnel or material, towards major projects, or individual organizations, which are really valid, which will really be capable to be part of a joint effort to pull Latin America from its present underdeveloped state.

Let us eliminate the risk of bewilderment, of waste of resources, of having to find out, when it is too late, that with the best of intentions, we were helping to conserve the present situation.

Our friends, especially from the United States, could render us a decisive collaboration for this effort by criticizing us, hammering on us whenever we became too pompous or formal, slow or inefficient. On the other hand, we would help them avoid headaches such as sending people to areas where they are not essential and will not receive proper material and spiritual assistance, or where they will run the risk of seeing such people become disappointed with themselves, their countries, or with our own countries; or channelling money into areas or organizations which will create new problems for us; or trying to export solutions which may have succeeded somewhere else but which will not prove solutions for our problems.

All of us together, the Latin American social movements and our friends, through planning and decision must proceed vigorously towards our ultimate goal: the integral development of a truly solidary continental civilization.

CHAPTER 7

Capitalism in Latin America

James A. Hart

The subject of capitalism in Latin America refers, of course, to a system of use and control of economic resources in which private individuals are free to own business enterprises and are free to control and manage them in accordance with the principle of freedom of enterprise. Now capitalism in this sense does not exist in Latin America, as indeed we well know.

The system in the United States does not represent pure capitalism anymore. We have heard in this country, and wisely so, of the excesses of capitalism. Even so, the United States today stands out as the most capitalist nation in the world. Canada probably ranks second in this regard.

But we leave North America and go to the 20 republics of the south. You walk into economic systems where the government has seen fit to curb the right of private ownership, to curb the rights of use of private resources, in a way which we still don't have here in the United States.

Only one of these countries, Cuba, has gone so far as to embrace the completely opposite system of economic arrangement, namely, communism. Under communism, of course, the state owns all resources. Cuba, as we well know, has not gone as far in this regard as Red China or the Soviet Union or the Soviet satellites of eastern Europe. But still it has embraced communism, a completely different system from ours.

VENEZUELA, ILLUSTRATION OF CAPITALISM The 19 other republics of Latin America lie much closer to us, of course, than they do to Cuba, but they are not capitalism as we know it. I'm going to discuss Venezuela as an illustration of capitalism in Latin America. It is not typical because no Latin American country is typical of all the others. Each one has its own individual personality. Each one has its own strengths and its own problems. Each one is different, as the countributors to this volume repeatedly emphasize. I think that if we understand Venezuela—as illustrative, not typical—we are in a better position to approach the other economies, the other capitalistic systems, when we see them.

To do this, I think a quick look at the history of Venezuela is in order. Venezuela, of course, was under Spanish dominion for many generations. The Spanish rule in Venezuela was no worse or no better than that in Latin America generally; and Venezuela like the other countries to the south of us, when Spain was conquered by Napoleon in the beginning of the last century, saw an opportunity to break away and it did so. It declared its independence on July 5th, 1811. At that time the patriots wrote a Declaration of Independence very similar to that of the United States.

In fact, they intended to declare their independence on the anniversary of ours, on July 4th of 1811. They weren't able to complete their business in time, so it was not until July 5th of 1811 that the declaration was made.

INDEPENDENCE DID NOT BRING PEACE   But even though Spain was displaced as despot, independence was not the beginning of peace and political tranquility in Venezuela. It was a long struggle. The war of independence itself lasted 10 years, and it was another 10 years, 1830, before Venezuela as we know it today became an independent, separate country. Before that it was linked with Panama, Colombia and Ecuador as Grand Colombia.

Even then, when it achieved its distinct independent status in 1830, Spanish despotism was simply replaced by domestic despotism. Year after year the Venezuelan people for the most part saw little change. The domestic despots were just as bad as the Spaniards, maybe worse. There were in all the history of Venezuela 26 different constitutions; the present constitution of 1961 represents the 26th. It has had revolutions on an average of once every two years. Until 1959, a mere six years ago, Venezuela never really knew or had a chance to appreciate democracy as we know it. During that time it had some of the worst dictatorships in the history of the world.

GOMEZ, NOTORIOUS DICTATOR   One in particular stands out because it helps to explain not only the present political picture in Venezuela but its economy as well. This man was Juan Vicente Gómez. Juan Vicente Gómez was vice-president under another Venezuelan tyrant dictator, President Cipriano Castro. President Cipriano Castro developed bad health and went to Europe for medical attention in 1908. He left his trusted vice-president Gómez behind. No sooner had his ship cleared the harbor and put out on the high seas than the trusted Gómez seized power. And he sent a message to the former dictator and said, "For the permanent good of your health, I suggest you stay permanently in Europe." And Castro followed that advice.

Thus began a 27-year long dictatorship which ranks certainly among the worst in the world. It's comparable to that of Josef Stalin of the Soviet Union and that lasted 29 years. They had much more in common than mere longevity. During this time a police state of the worst kind was established in Venezuela.

When the students protested in Venezuela, as they did frequently during his administration, he had a very simple technique. He simply arrested them, threw them in jail, and then took every tenth student and strung him up in a public place with a meathook through his neck. Even by the most tyrannical standards of the world Juan Vicente Gómez was one of the most crudely efficient dictators that the world has known.

OIL AND THE DICTATOR However, he was lucky because during his administration oil was discovered in Venezuela and by about 1920 it became a very important economic asset to the country. He lived until 1936 and died a natural death. They never deposed him. By 1936 oil was yielding for Venezuela a wealth that was undreamed of. It was so valuable that he was not only able to take care of all of the needs of the government, legitimate and otherwise, but he was able to abolish all taxes. For everything else that the Venezuelans suffered, at least it was a paradise for the taxpayers. Also, he was able to take care of himself and his friends and relatives out of this oil. When he died he left an estate of $200 million.

The important thing to remember about Gómez and his impact on today's economy and political life is that the young men of Gómez's day are the political leaders of today. They grew up under this dictatorship. They learned to hate. They learned to fight. And with a dictatorship of this kind it's no wonder that at times they went to extremes in their political activity. The present president of Venezuela, Leoni, was a student under Gómez. He was 60 years old in April of this year. He tells the story that when he first came to Caracas as a farm boy at the age of fifteen, he was impressed by his first carnival. He noticed, however, that this carnival kept moving in procession around a single building. The people were singing and dancing and having a gay time. But why, he inquired, did they keep going around this building? He found out; Gómez had political prisoners in that building and he deliberately sent carnivals down there to entertain themselves with great happiness so the people inside could be further tortured.

IMPORTANCE OF A DISTINGUISHED PROFESSOR During this period when Leoni was a student in Caracas, his predecessor as president, Betancourt, was likewise a student in the capital as were other political leaders. Gustavo Machado, the head of the Communist Party and twice its candidate for the presidency, was among them.

Ironically enough—and this is something which to teachers should be a great lesson—all of these men were under the guidance of one distinguished professor, Rómulo Gallegos. Rómulo Gallegos, the greatest, most distinguished novelist in the history of Venezuela, was running a school called the Liceo Caracas. He taught all of these young men. He was basically an atheist but he was dedicated to freedom for his people and to the elimination of racial prejudice. *Doña Bárbara,* his greatest novel, was translated into English thirty years ago. It ran into 20 editions in Spanish and was one of the all-time best sellers of the Spanish literary world. In all of these books he dwelt on the social suffering of the people of Venezuela and did it bravely. Many of his white characters married Negroes. He championed racial integration within his continent.

AFTERMATH OF GOMEZ   What happened after Gómez died? For one thing, Betancourt and Leoni came back. They had been students together. They had demonstrated together. Luckily they had not been hanged or shot by Gómez; they had gone into exile in Colombia. As a matter of fact, Leoni spent so much time in exile in Colombia that he even got his law degree at the University of Bogotá rather than in Caracas. When he and Betancourt first fled they were inseparable; they even operated a fruit stand together in Colombia. When they came back after the dictatorship, they began to organize the party which is the government party today, Democratic Action, known by the initials AD for *Acción Democrática.* They made a marvelous team of politicians— Betancourt the fiery speaker who could whip up a crowd and Leoni the quiet, behind-the-scene organizer. He established labor unions and built up committees in every state, territory and district of Venezuela. When in 1958 elections finally came for the first time in the history of Venezuela, Betancourt was the candidate of *Acción Democrática.* Leoni stayed behind the scenes and managed the campaign. In

CHAPTER 8

Agrarian Reform in Latin America
Hugo Jordan

The economic barometers of Latin America indicate that
agricultural development throughout the Latin American
region in the aggregate will not be possible until the out-
moded methods of agriculture are corrected and the rural
population is actually incorporated in the economic system.
They also reveal that the solution to this state of affairs can
be obtained only by intensive massive and radical measures
which will involve an economic, social, and technological
revolution in agricultural circles. An analysis of the indicators brings out the following fundamental characteristics
which mark in varying degrees the agricultural programs
of all the countries of Latin America.

CONCENTRATION OF OWNERSHIP   The first point is that there
is a concentration of ownership of agricultural resources. In
Latin America we have about 7½ million farm divisions.
Of these 7½ million, 100,000 account for 65 percent of all
the agricultural land in private hands. I wish to note that
these 100,000 possessors are less than 1½ percent of the
total; in other words, 1½ percent of the total farm parcels
comprise 65 percent of the total agricultural area. On the
other hand, 5½ million farms of less than 28 employees
contain less than 4 percent of this same area. In terms of
the active regional farm population this means that of a total
32 million people some 100,000 people own 471 million
acres. 1.9 million are medium size farmers and close to 30
million are landless farm workers.

111

CONCENTRATION AND ITS CONSEQUENCES The second fact is that the concentration of this ownership of the land creates a similar concentration of agricultural income.

The third statistic is that the large property holdings foster a further growth of inequality. The large area permits an income high enough to satisfy extensive needs of the owners. Laborers are compensated mainly through goods and services joined with a very low salary.

The fourth factor is that the large property does not favor development of technology to utilize better the abundant resources of man and land, and with greater efficiency utilize scarce resources.

A fifth consideration is that the concentration of land and income permits a concentration of economic and political power in the landholding minority.

Sixth, the concentration of income keeps the rural majorities almost totally out of the economic activity, limiting the development of other economic sectors. We should keep in mind that in 1960 the population of Latin America was estimated at 206 million people. Of these about 110 million were rural inhabitants. This creates a real problem for industry because these rural people do not have buying power as long as they are not incorporated into the economy. Without a buying power industry cannot develop.

Seventh, this concentration of economic and political power prevents the Latin American masses from participating freely and actively in the political process.

Eighth, the proliferation of landless families contributes to the deterioration of the situation. The income obtained from the small farm is very low and such farms do not provide steady work. Their limited area invites an extensive exploitation of the land. The lack of capital and the marginal operation of this type of farming impede the fostering of greater fertility to compensate for small land areas.

INADEQUATE SOLUTIONS Fundamentally the solution to the agrarian problem, termed land reform or agrarian reform, has been based on three criteria—economic, technical, and political. These criteria consider man as an object of the reform and not as its subject and principal agent. In general, the concept of agrarian reform is confined to the restructuring of land tenure. Its overall goals have been limited to complementary measures such as credit and technical assistance. It has been suggested that the modification of the present land tenure would in turn obtain the redistribution of farm income with its economic and political power.

Three massive Latin American land reforms have demonstrated the fallacy of this partial attempt. In not one of these three countries do the rural majorities today have more participation in those decisions which affect them directly, at local or national levels, than they had before. The revolutionary changes with their slogans of "land to the landless," "land and liberty," "land belongs to those who work it," have only served to change the power from the hands of the traditional minority to those of a new minority. The lopsided state and people relationship has remained intact if not strengthened. Those who ought to have been the subjects of the change were never consulted nor heard in the formulation of solutions. Nor were they invited to participate actively in the process. But, indeed, they were urged to be the participants in revolutionary events which served to change old masters for new masters.

LAND WITHOUT THE RIGHTS OF LANDOWNERS   The one party system in Mexico, for instance, and the one master system in Cuba, and the failure to communicate with the Bolivian Indians certainly are not indicative of the greater participation of beneficiaries in the political process through a more just social order or more equitable distribution of income. The landless, it is true, have gotten the land but not the corpus of rights that the ownership of the land should carry with it.

Our evaluation of the agrarian situation is that this constitutes not only an economic problem but that primarily it has a social character which cannot be analyzed independently from the global social reality of the region. This global nature in reality has two outstanding characteristics upon which the rural situation acts as a determining factor: an acute inadequacy between necessities and resources, and a state of pre-revolutionary tension. Although this is the result of a series of causes which are interrelated and mutually affected, we point out four of the important ones:

1) the extraordinary concentration of agricultural resources in a few hands;
2) the difficulty of incorporating the vast natural resources of the region into production due to insufficient economic development;
3) the low scientific and technological level which impedes significant increases in productivity;
4) the demographic explosion which shows the highest rate of population growth in the world and a high index of unemployment which is a cause of many explosive situations.

LITTLE REFORMS ARE NOT ENOUGH   These fundamental aspects characterize Latin American development and cause a state of pre-revolutionary tension. Facing these pressures which demand profound changes in the socio-economic structures, the majority of regional governments have reacted with a reformist attitude which in general has not touched the essence of the problem. These reforms have been called *reformitas,* that is, little reforms. The governments have intervened without consulting or asking for the participation of the people. With exterior pressures, these governments reluctantly assume the compromise of the Alliance for Progress and in the majority of cases they have ordered only those measures necessary to legitimize themselves before the United States and thus be able to continue receiving financial resources. The financial help channelled through the Alliance barring possible exceptions where it has gone to

private reform movements has continued favoring the traditional minorities in power which in general are not representative of the Latin American people. The Latin American
majorities, undermined by a feeling of failure and of nonful-
fillment, are irritated with minorities which have access to
power.

Our sociological interpretation of these facts is that a great
part of the Latin American population is in a marginal state
with respect to the process of development. This situation is
brought about because many Latin American societies do
not have a clear concept of their ultimate end and they
cannot have it because the people have not been called to
cooperate in the definition of the end nor have they been
consulted in the selection of measures and tasks which might
coordinate the different interests of the community. We
affirm that economic, technological and scientific requisites
are not enough in a process of development but that it is
necessary to consider the social organization in which the
action of the community is oriented toward the attainment
of a common end. Latin America does not have such a social
organization.

MAN MUST PARTICIPATE IN BUILDING SOCIETY It is necessary
to promote a national integration understood as the dynamic
participation of man in the construction of a society orientated to the common end of liberty and the common good
of society.

We do not believe that it would be possible to take the
farm population out of its marginal state unless measures
are taken in the agricultural area of development as well as
in the area of global development. In the area of global
development the most urgent and principal question is the
type of social reform needed to establish a social organization based on the principle of national integration so as to
incorporate segregated sectors and create a social system
which permits balanced development. This social reform
must promote the grass roots organizations of society from

the different economic sectors, coordinating and orienting them around a specific objective which directs them toward a common end.

At an intermediate level between the grass roots organizations and the government authority, structures must be created, specialized in their functions and coordinated locally, nationally and regionally, grouping the grass roots organizations around common ends.

The planning of global development with full participation of the majorities through its grass roots and intermediate organizations is fundamental.

HARMONIOUS REGIONAL DEVELOPMENT IS NECESSARY   Finally, the national structural reform must be complemented by an international integration in order to obtain harmonious regional development.

In the agricultural sector more than in any other sector the majority of the population is apart from the national life. Its participation in the productive process is reduced to the contribution of passive and servile labor in the lower strata of an extremely rigid social structure. Any change in the structure in Latin America must consider a radical reform as a fundamental and decisive element to assure the permanency of the change. In the sector which comprises more than half the population the majorities are weak in doctrinal conception and social organization. This makes it difficult to conceive that rural participation would share in the process of the reforms unless by anticipating these events we can assure that the radical reforms encounter a strong popular rural organization in the economic and the community aspects. It is in the rural sector where we must reinforce and expand the promotion of the popular movements.

The rural population lives mainly from agriculture and therefore is in a continual state of dependence. Discounting rare exceptions, the farm population has a level of life of mere subsistence with very limited culture and scarce technical skill. Under these conditions promotion directed toward the organization of movements cannot be positive if at the same time we do not provide the elements which permit the movements to prosper in the economic plane. These elements are technical and credit assistance.

Agriculture is the principal activity of the peasants. Therefore technical and credit assistance should be channelled mainly toward the betterment of the agricultural sector in order to obtain an improved economic foundation.

PROMOTION OF ORGANIZED SOLIDARITY Therefore under the term "promotion of rural movements" we understand three simultaneous, balanced, interdependent actions: the promotion of organized solidarity in the socio-economic sphere, technical assistance and credit assistance. None of these tasks can be carried out independently of the others without sacrificing the effectiveness of the overall action. It is important to emphasize the necessity of an adequate balance among these three actions. The promotion of community solidarity arouses in the peasant groups a desire to prosper. However, they find themselves without the tools with which to transform these desires into concrete realities of socio-economic betterment. This desire then turns into a negative situation feeding on a sense of frustration among the peasants who see the goals ahead but are without means to achieve them.

Community centers have as their foundation the principle of subsidiarity between the state and the private sector and similarly between the private sector and individuals.

The actions which the private sector may exercise with efficiency through its organizations within the framework of the common good of the nation should not be assumed by the state but turned over to this sector in the measure that its organizations can assist progress.

In the present case this subsidiarity is organized through grass roots organizations, intermediary bodies and larger organizations at the national, territorial or local level. Considering the weaknesses of the rural majorities and that their organizations are small and ineffective, no more than very elementary tasks could be delegated to them.

This vacuum is overcome by the community centers whose purpose is to make up for the weaknesses noted above, providing those services which the organizations cannot provide. In order to promote rural development it is necessary to multiply the rural community centers with emphasis on the socio-economic field so that there can be an economic base in the form of credit and technical assistance.

RECOGNIZE "THE LATIN AMERICAN MAN" Latin America is not only a geographic region but constitutes a unit formed by a common historic past and common culture. The Latin American man is a distinct reality. He has his own characteristics which are different from others in the world. The solutions to the Latin American problems in the social, economic, political and cultural aspects cannot be imported but must be searched for by Latin Americans in accord with the Latin American reality.

The above implies that the promotion of the popular movements must be the result of a sequence which begins with the investigation of the reality of the region. Only in the measure that this methodical examination is attained will it be possible to provide priorities, territorial or categorical. However, to this rather rigid outline we have to add an element that gives it flexibility and urgency. Actually the state of pre-revolutionary tension to which we have referred has not affected all countries of the region in an equal manner. In some countries fundamental changes have already occurred and in others these processes are developing or being initiated. Due to this circumstance any progress must have extreme mobility and agility.

A PLEA TO HUSBAND AVAILABLE RESOURCES On the other hand, we must realize the fact that the financial resources will always be insufficient in the face of the magnitude of the problems of development and this makes it necessary to consider very strongly the cost-benefit relationship. It is difficult to determine precisely how much money has arrived to Latin America from the outside Christian world to aid the temporal efforts of the Latin American Church. We know, however, that the sum totals millions of dollars. By ignoring basic considerations an erroneous sense of charity has wasted many resources in projects badly conceived and badly operated.

It is true that until recent years the temporal action of the Latin American Church was developed without national or regional organization or coordination, but this has changed. In 1961 the Center for Economic and Social Development for Latin America was created—DESAL.

THE FUNCTION OF DESAL   DESAL is a private institution whose objective is the investigation of the Latin American problems of development and the promotion of solutions at the popular level. This objective determines the following specific tasks:

1) elaboration of needs;
2) planning and programming of the action of promotion;
3) creation of the mechanism of promotion at the national level;
4) coordination of the action of promotion at the regional level;
5) channelling of resources for the mechanism of promotion and for the movements themselves;
6) evaluation and promotion of specific projects.

ACCOMPLISHMENTS OF DESAL   Since its foundation the work of DESAL in the national mechanism can be summarized as follows:

1) Countries attended: fourteen (Mexico, Guatemala, Panama, Colombia, Venezuela, Ecuador, Peru, Bolivia, Chile, Paraguay, Uruguay, Argentina, Haiti, Dominican Republic).

2) Specific projects promoted: 475
   a. socio-economic projects, 213
   b. social service centers, 137
   c. community development projects, 78
   d. national institutes of development, 12
   e. regional institutes, 5
   f. a Latin American family life center
   g. a Latin American confederation for basic education
   h. a university seminar program

Pertaining to the rural community proper, the task accomplished can be appreciated by the following rural movements and rural centers. (These are included in the above figures.)

1) socio-economic projects, 72
2) community development projects, 41
3) social service centers, 49
4) rural centers, 11

The funds assigned to these projects amount to $13,150,-000. Approximately 82 percent of these funds have come from Europe, many from German and Belgian foundations. Eighteen percent have been provided by the United States of America through the Agency for International Development, the Institute for Human Progress, International Development Foundation, Ford Foundation and some private groups.

It can be seen that in Latin America we have a regional institutional structure based on a clear doctrinal conception and intimate knowledge of reality which has carried on a positive promotion of popular movements in the rural sector. The logic of our planning and the efficiency developed in the operation has been recognized by the European Christian world and by international agencies for economic and social development. These have channelled important financial resources for the further promotion of rural movements.

As far as we are aware, the participation of the North

American Catholic world in the financing of our action has been extremely limited. On first thought, there would be a justification for this limited participation. As citizens of the United States, you are contributing to the development of Latin America through the Alliance for Progress. The fundamental goal of the Alliance, as the late President Kennedy so dramatically explained, is to combat misery, hunger, and illiteracy; in sum, to free the Latin American poor.

IS THE ALLIANCE ACCOMPLISHING ITS OBJECTIVE? But as citizens of this country, have you asked yourself whether the Alliance is accomplishing its objective? This question can only be answered by acquainting yourselves with the Latin American world and analyzing the causes of its reality. If you do this, you will find that the Alliance for Progress is not accomplishing its goal and that it will not fulfill it unless the context of the inter-American cooperation is fully revised. In fact, as long as the Alliance is maintained in terms of a program from the *government* of the United States to the *governments* of Latin America, its objective will be fulfilled only in those cases where these latter are *true* representatives of the majority. But almost all Latin American governments represent a traditional minority. Is it possible to suppose that these minorities who for generations have possessed and defended the land and economic and political power would use the Alliance to surrender this power? In these circumstances is it possible that the Organization of American States whose components are *named* by these governments truly represent the Latin American majorities?

THE RESPONSIBILITY TO MAKE RIGHT DECISIONS These questions contain profound implications but, nevertheless, we feel we cannot avoid facing them. Thousands of your citizens have gallantly given their lives on the battle fronts of faraway lands, defending the freedom of other people. Latin America is today the battlefield of a war, cold but cruel and violent. It is a war between many millions of beings who have neither liberty nor bread or shelter and millions who have everything. We cannot be neutral in this war. We have taken our side with the oppressed. We believe that you as Catholics and as citizens of this country, the champion of liberty and democracy, should also decide with whom you side. We need your cooperation to narrow the gap between the necessities and the financial resources.

There is not much time left to structure the cooperation which we are searching for. Latin America is rapidly approaching fundamental decisions which will affect the whole hemisphere. That these definitions may have the doctrinal context that we profess is not only our responsibility; we feel that it is also yours.

CHAPTER 9

Christians and Workers' Movements

William C. Doherty, Jr., the first director of the American Institute for Free Labor Development (AIFLD), presented at the CICOP conference in Chicago the expanding program of labor education in Latin America which is a source of such deep satisfaction to so many trade unionists of the United States. Mr. Doherty's statement constitutes the first part of this chapter.

Since the Latin American speaker engaged to present the development of the Confederation of Latin American Christian Trade Unionists (CLASC) could not participate at the CICOP conference, we quote as second part of this chapter from an article on CLASC published in the spring of 1965 by International Federation of Christian Trade Unions whose headquarters are in Brussels.

I am a Christian. I am a Catholic, and I'm very proud of that fact. At Catholic University and at Georgetown I have read and studied the encyclicals, subscribed to the theories as expressed therein, and tried to apply them in my personal life and in my organizational life. I am also a North American trade unionist, and I am equally proud of that. I sometimes have difficulties deciding where Caesar's role begins and where it ends, but I think that all of us have that problem on occasion. I've been given a great pleasure during the course of the last 15 years of my life in that it has been devoted to the international labor movement. I had the privilege of living and working in Latin America during the course of the past ten years. I lived in Mexico City for close to four years and for several years in Brazil. I have six children, three of whom were born in Latin America. And I feel, therefore, that I am at least half Latin American. So in addition to the other things that I am, I consider myself a great friend of Latin America and for that reason I am proud to be here this afternoon. I think this CICOP conference is a tremendous event, and I think this is the type of conference that could not have been held here in the city of Chicago five years ago. I sometimes don't know whether I give John Kennedy most of the credit for that or Fidel Castro. Probably they both have to share the responsibility, the blame or the credit; but nevertheless we're here and it's important that we be here.

NEW ATMOSPHERE FOR LABOR   Eight years ago I was organizing unions in Latin America. In one particular country, Guatemala, I was trying to organize a subsidiary of the United Fruit Company. I was not permitted to go into Guatemala at that time by the government of Ydígoras Fuente because I was accused of being the chief communist agent for Central America and, as such, a dangerous element working among the workers of Central America. It took personal intervention by then Under Secretary of State, Robert Murphy, to convince the President of Guatemala that I was not a communist. Now eight years later not only myself but literally dozens of American trade unionists can work throughout Latin America without this accusation being held over their heads. I think this is significant of the change that has taken place in Latin America.

I have had the privilege of organizing workers and unions and organizing strikes, some of which have lasted as many as 90 days, in order to get recognition for unions, winning strikes and losing strikes in Latin America. I had the pleasure of writing and seeing signed the first collective bargaining agreement in the whole communications industry of Brazil. I feel that I have shared many happy moments and many sad moments with the workers of Latin America. I understand their needs, their appetites, their desires and some of the fears that are prevalent in that part of the world. I think in order to properly understand many of the fine talks that we've heard here today and throughout the course of the week and will hear in the future that there has to be a better understanding of the labor movement of the Western Hemisphere. There are many misrepresentations of the U.S. trade union point of view rampant in the world today, and if you'll bear with me, I'd like to make a brief analysis of the labor movement—perhaps more quantitative than qualitative, but I don't have much time.

FORTY-TWO MILLION TRADE UNIONISTS There are approximately 42 million organized trade union members in the Western Hemisphere, if we were to give to the claimants the total membership which they assert. If we were to use a criterion of dues-paying, paid up membership as we do in the United States, probably it would be considered to be an inflated figure. There are within the Western Hemisphere four general broad classifications within which the unions to which these 42 million souls belong fall. I might add that if you take the conservative figure of giving four mouths to each bread-winner, and I repeat that is conservative because our Latin American friends like my own family which is Irish are rather prolific, you'll see that we're talking about 60 million people. This is substantial when you talk in terms of the effect of the labor movement whether it be in the United States or in Latin America. This is why this afternoon's speakers, I think, to a man or to a lady refer first to the labor movement as being a significant force with which we have to deal when talking about social change.

Of that 42 million about 30 million associate themselves with an organization known as ORIT, the *Organización Regional Interamericana de Trabajadores*. Of that 30 million within the ranks of ORIT, about 15 million are in Latin America and about 15 million are in the United States and Canada or in North America.

There are another 5 million workers, both in unions and

in campesino leagues, which are claimed by the CLASC, the Latin American Christian Confederation of Workers. There are perhaps another 5 million workers in Latin America who are in independent unions, which are not affiliated with either the ORIT or the CLASC or with the latter group which we would give conservatively, or maybe generously, 2 million members, namely the Communists with the Communist International known as the CTAL, the *Corporación de Trabajadores de América Latina*.

NON-DENOMINATIONAL UNIONS The American Federation of Labor and the Congress of Industrial Organization along with the United Mine Workers and the Canadian Labor Congress are affiliated to the ORIT. The ORIT is a non-denominational trade union grouping. The AFL-CIO never has, does not today, and never will take the second seat to anyone in terms of its defense of the Judao-Christian ethic and the papal encyclicals. However, the pluralistic concept of society as we experience it in the United States at times does not permit other than the personal identification with the papal encyclicals. This is often misunderstood outside the United States. This does not mean that at the leadership level within the ranks of the masses and the members there is not dedication to the Christian principle. It is there. It is just that it cannot be made institutionally manifest or it would destroy the whole ecumenical, if you will, or pluralistic concept of society as we know it.

Now, in Latin America where at least 95% of the population is Catholic the situation is quite different. Open and widely known association with the principles of the encyclicals in an institutional manner is not only possible but highly desirable.

There are other misunderstandings rampant in the world regarding the North American labor movement or the so-called ORIT block and capitalism as it exists today. There is often an attempt to associate out-of-hand the North American labor movement and the ORIT or International

Trade Secretariat membership with Victorian capitalism, with the capitalistic countries or the capitalistic societies. This is a stereotyped view of the situation because it avoids a description of what we mean by capitalism in 1965, what we meant by it in 1900, and what we will probably mean by it in the year 2000. In order to adequately portray the concept of the American labor movement with regard to capitalism, I'm going to ask you to bear with me for a very brief moment.

U.S. LABOR AND PRIVATE ENTERPRISE   In 1963 President George Meany, who incidentally is a Catholic, stated the official policy position of the American Federation of Labor and Congress of Industrial Organizations and I would dare say was probably representative of the attitude of the over-whelming majority of the labor unions associated with the AFL-CIO in Latin America when he issued a statement as follows:

American labor has always wholeheartedly supported our private enterprise system. Under this system our country has obtained the highest living standard in the world. Moreover, the labor movement has found that it can best protect the interest of the workers in a free economy as it exists in the United States. However, our economic system is possible only within the larger framework of a democratic society which has developed strong countervailing forces to private capitalism. These forces include free trade unions and free collective bargaining, farmer and consumer organizations, a congress that acts as a watchdog in cases of abuse of economic power, anti-trust laws, social legislation, regulatory agencies, and the like.

As a result the laissez-faire economy of the 19th century has been changed into the "mixed economy" prevailing today in the United States as in most other industrially advanced countries of the world.

But these countervailing forces do not exist in most underdeveloped countries. Not only political democracy but the national state as such is still in its infancy. Labor is numerically weak and farmers or consumer organizations are almost non-existent. Parliament is controlled by a strong executive. The one party system is common. Social legislation, if there is any, is better on paper than in practice. In such circumstances the chances for an emulation of the remarkable success and progress of our own economic system are, to say the least, dim. There is, on the contrary, an acute danger that we will witness a repetition of the exploitation and the anti-labor practices which threatened America in the early years of the Industrial Revolution. In too many instances private capital in the new nations has been interested solely in making big profits fast with no regard for the long-term economic development of the country let alone working and living conditions of the workers.

America's objectives should be free societies, politically free, with the ultimate power in the hands of the people. That is the basic point. The people may choose to concentrate on government ownership, control and planning. That is up to them. They may also want a greater degree of private enterprise. That is also up to them. This country's concern should only be that the choice is freely made and that the choice can be freely altered. Only the Soviet Union and its satellites attempt to impose their economic system on other nations. We should not try to imitate them.

I would submit that in the true sense of the word as utilized by Bishop McGrath that *that* represents the revolution which we of the American trade union movement are working for in Latin America. I would also submit that I see nothing whatsoever out of consort between the philosophy as expressed in that statement and the mystique as expressed in that statement and that of Christian Democracy as I know it in its differing forms from country to country throughout Latin America.

U.S. LABOR AND L.A. LABOR   Now, what have we done in a

practical way within the workers' movement—the labor movement—in order to bring assistance to our friends in Latin America? If I may, and again bearing in mind the time limitation, I would like to state that we have long enjoyed traditional relationships with our friends in the labor movement to the south. As a matter of fact, the founding father of the American trade union movement, Samuel Gompers, first visited Mexico in 1921 in an exchange of views with the Mexican labor movement and died on his return to Washington from that visit to Mexico. And from that early date on we have had, with varying degrees of emphasis and determination, relations with the trade union movement of Latin America. It was in truth, however, only after World War II that the American labor movement—and I might add, long before the advent of Fidel Castro who at times, without being too cynical and without losing sight of the suffering of our friends in Cuba, we have to be thankful for because work in Latin America now goes forward at a much more rapid rate—but in 1947 and 1948 the American trade union movement had representatives in Latin America helping to organize unions *not* patterned, as many say, after the U.S. model but patterned after the desires and the appetites of very intelligent workers in Latin America who know full well what they need. Through the International Trade Secretariats, the ORIT, and through independent associations we have helped with money, with materials, with men, with ideas and with hard work to organize and form unions throughout Latin America because we know that there is a social revolution going on in Latin America and we're trying to help that be a democratic revolution. We also know that there is no social justice in Latin America or any place in the world without unions. We know that the worker, if he gets it on a silver platter, is living in some form of a paternalistic state. He's got to earn it. He's got to have a union. He's got to demand it, and it's got to be his as a matter of right and prerogative. And the only way that can happen is through the free trade union movement. We know that there can be no political democracy without unions. We know that behind the Iron Curtain there are no unions and there is dictatorship. We know that in Franco's Spain there are no unions and there is dictatorship. We know that in Cuba, in Haiti, and in Paraguay there are no free unions and there are dictatorships. And we do not want these dictatorships in the countries where they do not now exist. And this is why we work with increasing fervor in terms of bringing the benefits of trade union organization to the workers of Latin America.

AMERICAN INSTITUTE FOR FREE LABOR DEVELOPMENT Two and a half years ago the American labor movement in revolutionary but pluralistic cooperation with the United States government and the United States business community formed a non-profit institution known as the American Institute for Free Labor Development and that institute now gives me the wherewithal to feed my family. The American Institute for Free Labor Development was formed under the concept that we could go into Latin America with massive education programs and bring the word, the mystique of free trade unionism, to the workers of Latin America by simultaneously going in and educating. We have now had in excess of 20,000 students through the courses that the American Institute offers in some 20 countries of Latin America with 13 residential institutes. We have had 295 students to Washington, D.C., for three month courses, a third of whom then go to Europe for a visit to Germany, to Italy, to England and to Israel for further training. The trade union movement is growing by leaps and bounds as a result of the training that these people have received.

THE SOCIAL PROJECTS DEPARTMENT However, we've also initiated a Social Projects Department because we saw that unless we could bring technical assistance to the unions of Latin America the often repeated promises that the unions would be able to participate in the Alliance for Progress would go to nought. We do not believe that development can take place with all of the U.S. taxpayer's wherewithal and donations and contributions and loans to the field of economic development if they all go down on a government to government basis because of the simple fact that many governments that claim to be representative of the people in Latin America are not and because of the simple fact that many of the aid funds never trickle down to the workers. So we have helped the unions of Latin America organize themselves into a position where they can get this assistance directly—not gifts, not doles, not grants, but by loans. We have sent our own engineers and technicians and architects and economists and sociologists and financial experts into Latin America, into every country of Latin America, organizing teams that can help the unions formulate feasible loan propositions in Washington for low cost housing, for hospitals, for consumers' cooperatives, for credit unions, for workers' banks (many of which are now functioning throughout Latin America). We have helped them prepare their loan applications and have now in a short two years arranged $130 million worth of credit line for the unions of Latin America, $67 million of which, by the way, comes from the American trade union movements, the welfare funds of the American unions. Not all of these funds are invested in the shoddy way in which you at times read in the newspapers because unfortunately the good things of the American labor movement do not get into the press of the United States. The $67 million of our own money represents a significant effort to help the workers of Latin America live better. These loans which we have engineered and assisted the unions of Latin America to receive have also been operating on a pluralistic basis. Less than half of the unions that have received our assistance are affiliated with the ORIT, despite what might have been heard to the contrary.

PROGRAM IN NORTHEAST BRAZIL In northeast Brazil we are assisting a whole program of rural labor development with four technicians that we already have on the scene: a trade unionist, a cooperative expert, an agricultural economist and an agricultural engineer in Recife. The rural labor movement of the Northeast, organized originally by the círculos operarios, represents a tremendous effort on the part of the Catholic Church to get into the field of campesino development. They've completely stolen the thunder from Francisco Juliao, the Communist League's campesinist. This Catholic effort has over 200,000 organized workers in their ranks, and our people are working hand in hand day by day with Father Melo and Father Crespo in an effort to establish campesino service centers wherein we teach marketing methods, fertilization, irrigation, and the technical know-how of 20th century farming because land reform is not enough.

This and many, many other efforts are being carried on in the field of social development by the American Institute for Free Labor Development, and recently we've established a Community Services Department so that we can care for the human element so that we don't just go down and build a lot of buildings and a lot of institutions which frankly had as their ultimate end the material progress of people. But where we can we help them maintain those institutions and resist exploitation from either foreign exploitation or domestic exploitation and build real democracy at the grass roots. This, in the brief time allotted to me, is the record of the American labor movement to date in Latin America.

JOSE MARTI AND AIFLD   We consider José Martí of Cuba to be one of the great political philosophers of Latin America. He had some advice that many of us leaders of the American Institute for Free Labor Development take to heart and try to practice in Latin America. He was the Abraham Lincoln of Latin America. He could coin a phrase. At one time he said as he observed the world, *"El mundo se divide en dos ramas: los que aman y fundan, los que odian y destruyen."*—"The world divides itself into two branches: those who love and build, those who hate and destroy." We like to think we are loving and we like to think we are building.

A STATEMENT CONCERNING CLASC

A CALL FOR CONSIDERATION OF CLASC   At the CICOP conference in Chicago, as soon as Mr. Doherty completed this presentation of the work of ORIT in Latin America, Bishop Prata of La Paz, Bolivia, asked for the floor. "I appreciated very much the wonderful explanation Mr. Doherty gave," he said, "but please forgive me if I voice a little criticism. We are here to discuss the topic 'Christians and the Workers' Movements' and we had the idea that we would hear from the different movements. I would appreciate a word of explanation."

Father García of the Central American University followed Bishop Prata. "I see that CLASC isn't here," he said, "This is a Christian movement and apparently hasn't been invited. Why is it that CLASC and ORIT, both of which are labor movements, do not mingle in Latin America? Where CLASC and ORIT work in Latin America I have seen that CLASC criticizes ORIT very strongly. I would like to know why."

The CICOP program committee tried hard to have a presentation of CLASC at the conference but did not succeed. To many men of experience, the bitter controversy between the two movements threatens to play into the hands of the leftists.

THE ORIGINS OF CLASC   In 1954 Christian Democratic elements established a labor confederation for the purpose of coordinating Christian trade union activity throughout Latin America. This organization, the Confederation of Latin American Christian Trade Unionists (CLASC), early became the regional affiliate of the International Confederation of Christian Trade Unionists which claims membership of some millions, two-thirds of whom are in Europe. Its world headquarters are in Brussels, Belgium. Christian trade unionists of Europe have shown great sympathy for CLASC.

"For most of the opponents, CLASC is an insignificant group, not worth while talking about," states N. Leynse on the ORIT-CLASC controversy in the English-language edition of *Labor* (Issue Number 2, 1965), the house organ of the International Federation of Christian Trade Unions. "Yet, these last two years more paper and ink have been used up in writing on CLASC than about any other organization."

It is the contention of the International Federation of Christian Trade Unions that forces from the United States sought to block the entry of the IFCTU into Latin America. The first representative of that organization to carry on in Latin America was expelled as a communist agent and U.S. influence was blamed.

"Yet we were not destroyed," observes Leynse, "we have grown up to be a movement that embodies the hope in a better future in all the countries of Latin America."

THE FINANCING OF CLASC   European sources have of late supplied considerable funds for the development of CLASC.

"The largest part of this money," explains Leynse, "and the whole budget of aid to organizations comes from the Solidarity Fund of the IFCTU, while a great part of the action in the field of education is co-financed by the German (Christian) Foundation 'International Solidarity.' But one should not think that only Christian-social activities are financed by German funds. Social-democratic services also, and in Latin America the groups linked with ORIT, the Interamerican Regional Trade Union, receive German support."

ANTI-U.S.A. SPIRIT IN CLASC UNITS   Leynse takes note of the charge that CLASC unions are often anti-U.S.A. and explains it this way:

CLASC is as anti-USA as the average Latin American is. The members of the CLASC belong to the weaker and poorer part of the Americas. They thus feel a nearly inevitable reserve towards the richer part, all the more in that they can ascertain every day the ascendancy of the richer part as well in the inter-American institutions as in their respective countries. The power of the USA investments in Latin America, their frequent supremacy over the national capital, their as frequent alliance with the representatives of the Latin American feudal structures, all that creates a nearly inevitable reaction of antipathy in the average man.

If the Soviet Union, or any other foreign power had in Latin America an economic power comparable to that of the USA, then they would bump into the same reaction.

Far be it from us to assert that this unpleasant feeling is always and everywhere justified. It certainly is not and it is a fact that the USA investments have contributed much, still contribute and will have to contribute, to the development of the economic activity in Latin America.

That the resentment resulting from these situations, which do exist, is directed against the North Americans without any distinction, is perhaps to be deplored, but can hardly be denied. It is moreover a general feeling that did not originate since the growth of the CLASC, and whose instigator CLASC was, but a feeling that goes back to a far-away past.

Finally this: that the self-consciousness of the Latin Americans as such grew at the same time throughout the whole of the continent, and that this did not make the relationship with the USA any easier or milder is clear.

CLASC OPPOSITION TO FREE ENTERPRISE In contrast to the strong support most North American unionists give to free enterprise, CLASC unionists are known for their contrary stand. Lynse seeks to explain this:

CLASC is accused of being against free enterprise. But the CLASC has to be against free enterprise as it thrives everywhere in Latin America for the moment. This free enterprise does not give the workers their rightful share

of better living conditions. It is all too often in the hands
of those who want to maintain the present feudal institutions. CLASC wants the enterprises to be intent upon the
welfare of the population and not upon support of the
already privileged groups. That kind of free enterprise that
keeps the Latin American countries in a state of semi-
colonialism cannot in the long run be accepted by the
citizens of Latin America.

CLASC AND THE INTER-AMERICAN SYSTEM   Leynse notes that
CLASC is said to be against the inter-American system.
"But in the present form of this system," he asserts, "there
is on one side a number of relatively powerless Latin Ameri-
can countries and on the other side the mighty USA. The
CLASC wants most of all that a certain balance be realized
in regard to the USA through a strong Latin American unity.
The USA themselves are a confederation, they are the
United States."

CLASC AND VIOLENT REVOLUTION   Then there is the charge
that CLASC favors a violent revolution. Says Leynse:

"CLASC has always pronounced itself in favor of revolutionary structural reforms in Latin America. With this
it finds itself in the company of the late President Kennedy
and of Arturo Moscoso. To assert that the CLASC system-
atically calls for violence is an obvious lie. The 'revolution in freedom' President Frei promised to the Chileans
corresponds completely to the conceptions of the CLASC.
"And so the last and easiest step against the CLASC is
rapidly taken: the CLASC is pro-communist. We remember here the first reactions against the Christian trade-
union in Latin America. Those who want to kill off every
dynamic movement against exploitation, repression and
social injustice with the clincher of communism play a
game as dangerous as criminal. What will they say when
one day the people will believe them and consider the
communists as the only hard fighters for social justice?
"The CLASC wants to give a new hope to the Latin

American proletariat with the revolutionary contents of this Christianity of ours with its fierce demands for justice. This hope implies: real freedom, justice, participation in responsibility and in welfare, elimination of privilege and of feudal laws of property and authority. We can only be thankful that at last a group of Christians fights as grimly for these true values as the communists fight for their delusions. The slander that the CLASC is pro-communist can fall on good ground only among the most backward and reactionary groups of Latin America."

UNION HANDICAPS IN LATIN AMERICA "A mere bread and butter trade union has no future in Latin America or in any developing area of the globe. The Latin American farm and industrial workers need a large syndical action that pursues basic structural reforms on the social and economic level as an essential condition to a rapid and lasting development of the standards of living and the spiritual and cultural liberation of the workers.

"It is evident that the trade union must use all the possibilities and advantages that collective labor agreements can offer. But we put two positive questions in this context:

1) In how many countries of Latin America is the free and independent trade union—including the Christian union—really recognized and accepted by employers and authorities as a full partner and representative of the workers?
2) In what measure is the trade union independent of employees and authorities to the point that it has the possibility to negotiate?

"The CLASC is not opposed to free enterprise in the modern sense, but it is opposed to liberal capitalism, that uses the principle of free enterprise to keep the workers poor and to make the rich even richer. That is the reality in many Latin American countries."

A PLEA FOR RECOGNITION OF CLASC "It seems to us that enough time has been wasted in sterile quarrels. We think that an open and honest recognition of CLASC in Latin America is necessary, as the CLASC is one of the wings of a truly free trade unionism in Latin America. With a minimum of good faith and goodwill, cooperation between all the various free democratic forces in Latin America and between these Latin American forces and those of the USA should be possible.

"Here lies the future of the whole continent if one wants to safeguard it against communism."

RAMON VENEGAS AND THE GREAT MISUNDERSTANDING   Mr. Ramón Venegas, the eminent Chilean architect, Secretary General of the Center for Economic Development of Latin America (DESAL), made a thoughtful observation at the CICOP conference in Chicago:

I would like to observe just one thing. I don't want to speak about CLASC or ORIT or similar matters. I don't think that these represent the problem.

The problem is that you, the North Americans, are in a society absolutely different from our society. We need revolution; you don't need revolution. It is impossible that you, here in this society, should comprehend what we need.

Every one of our movements, in our opinion, needs a doctrine that is very clear, very explicit to act by. We need political parties with ideological positions. We need trade unions with very clear doctrinal positions. I am not speaking of confessionalism, of a Catholic or Protestant stand for a trade union or a cooperative. I speak of a social philosophy to fight injustice with justice, to replace misery with well being. In these things we cannot be neutral. This is the great misunderstanding between us.

CHAPTER 10

Christian Participation in
National Planning

René Otero

ORIGIN OF THE IDEA OF PLANNING It may truly be said that the idea of planning for the development of Latin America was born of the conviction that 19th century economic and political liberalism was unable to generate economic and social growth at the rate required and that to achieve such growth it became evident that the need existed for planning the unification of available resources. In many of the world's financial centers, especially in the United States, this reaction was thought to be a manifestation of an extremist outlook calling for intervention by the state in economic and social processes of the nation, and it was supported neither by government nor by entities which could serve as possible sources of financing for development.

It was not until the United States had experienced the severe economic and social problems accompanying the economic depression of the 30's that the importance of a central authority exercising some supervision of economic activity was recognized. The depression brought about a radical change in popular and official attitudes in the United States leading to greater participation by the federal government in the management of the economic process and illuminating the need for initiating programs for development and social welfare to alleviate the condition of the impoverished masses.

139

GREATLY ENLARGED PROGRAMS REQUIRED PLANNING   This evolution in the concept of the role of the state in economic and
social development as applied to Latin America signifies a
more realistic view of Latin America's problems and of the
urgency for cooperation in the economic and social growth
of the nation with greater emphasis being placed on multi-
lateral action. It was understood, too, that the best method
of achieving rapid and sustained economic growth and providing general social improvement for the people was to
carry on this activity, whether undertaken by the public or
by the private sector, within a well defined framework which
could be financed under conditions suitable to the situation
of each country.

The communist policy instituted by Castro shortly after
his assumption of power was undoubtedly a factor hastening
the acceptance of these principles long supported by politicians and economists in institutions representative of Latin
America.

DEEP CRISES BROUGHT PLANNING   Another important factor
in the determination of Latin America to insist on planned
economic and social development was that the Latin American economy in general has experienced marked growth,
particularly during the last two decades. But serious crises
have frequently arisen during this development, the solution
of which was to slow this trend. It has been noted that
growth has been uneven among the various social sectors to
the extent that most Latin Americans have enjoyed only a
limited share of its benefits. Moreover, if we observe the
high rate of population growth which is present precisely
among the least favored classes of society, we shall find that
year after year the number of the unprivileged grows at a
faster rate than that of the beneficiaries of development.

Under such circumstances the need to institutionalize the
planning and programming of development becomes apparent as a requirement for any sound economic policy and for
obtaining financial resources. This effort culminated with the

holding of two important inter-American meetings. The first of these two was the meeting of the Committee of the Twenty-one at Bogotá in September 1960 where the member countries of the inter-American system signed the Act of Bogotá which constitutes "a total effort to raise the standard of living and social conditions of the peoples of the hemisphere." The second was the extraordinary meeting of the inter-American economic and social council at Punta del Este in August 1961 where the Charter of Punta del Este was signed establishing the Alliance for Progress.

PUNTA DEL ESTE AND PLANNING   It is worthwhile to recall that in the Charter of Punta del Este appears the requirement "that comprehensive and well conceived national planning of economic and social development aimed at the achievement of self-sustained growth be carried out in accordance with democratic principles." In this regard it should be noted that since the Act of Bogotá the interdependence between social and economic development has been firmly acknowledged as an accepted principle by all the countries of the inter-American system.

We may say, then, that it is an officially accepted principle that economic growth and social development in Latin America will be accomplished more rapidly and more effectively through national and regional development planning. This principle will be even more widely accepted as experience accrues to the agencies responsible for assistance in the preparation of this planning.

CHRISTIAN PARTICIPATION IN SOCIAL PLANNING   To situate Christians particularly in national planning within this framework we must make it very clear that the contribution of the United States to economic and social development efforts in Latin America has at present been primarily made through the mechanism of the Alliance for Progress.

Is there a place for the concept of Christian participation in social planning? We will make a brief analysis of the elements of such Christian participation.

From a pragmatic point of view we can say that by Christian participation in the planning of development we mean the integration of the efforts and resources of the Christian organizations of a country or of a continent with those of the social community to achieve a balanced improvement of the standard of living of the people.

First of all, we as Christians base our effort in this strictly material sphere on a precept or mandate given by God himself when he ordered the human race to increase, multiply, and subdue the earth, because when man controlling nature, puts into use all the resources of creation and transforms them into economic and cultural goods his activity becomes part of God's basic plan. Further, the Christian who works for the economic and social development of his fellow man, who concerns himself with providing better living conditions for mankind through the exploitation of natural resources, will be able to offer to God a more developed world, a world closer to perfection, because "in order that creation might sing with Jesus Christ the glory of God by the sacrificial offering of all Christians, they must first have taken possession of creation."

CONCERN FOR DEVELOPMENT OF PEOPLE   This mandate calls upon us to acknowledge the importance of considering as part of the divine plan and as an important duty of Christians this concern for the economic and social development of the people. We are, then, faced with the task, the execution of which is clearly and unequivocally demanded. However, it is well to ask ourselves two questions. Are we Christians prepared to share in the effort for the development of Latin America effectively and enduringly, so as to make the fruits of that development permanent and to assure its continuing growth? Or are we wasting our efforts and resources in a diffused movement impelled only by a provisional outlook toward Latin American problems?

Before attempting to answer these questions we should make it clear that for the present we shall concern ourselves only with aspects of social development in its narrow significance since, though many opportunities exist for Christian participation in the strictly economic planning, that area would require another approach which does not fall within the scope of this presentation.

It is indisputable that Christians, always inspired by the social doctrine of the Church, have concerned themselves with social injustices and with the basic needs of the poor, acting through a range of organizations known as the social apostolate. But the present situation with the urgency of problems requiring immediate solutions and with the danger of attractive offers from other groups demands of us much more than that. Recently Christian activity has taken one or more steps in the right direction. A promising movement inspired by the hierarchy has begun in the conducting in Latin America of socio-economic studies and research through the establishing of various entities for this purpose. In the majority of cases, however, these efforts tend to be limited to inadequate social activity.

PLANS FOR PRAGMATIC ACTION   The world today requires much more. It demands of the Christian a more active and significant involvement in the life of the people and particularly of the poor. A two-fold goal must be attained: 1) categoric alleviation of poverty and squalor; 2) the rebirth of the community as human beings with body and soul. This will be achieved if in addition to the program for renewed pastoral activity that the bishops and clergy are carrying out so zealously, the Christian layman involves himself in effective participation in planning the economic and social development of fellow Christians.

Here it is well to note that pastoral planning is a special function of the Church, carried out by total mobilization of the needed human elements under Church control. Instead, in planning social development, the Christian must relate his work to the state as guardian of the common good, obliged to make certain that all benefits of contemporary life reach every segment of society.

We as Christians can make a real contribution to the efforts of our nations to achieve social advance in Latin America. This contribution can be made on two levels—that of the planning itself and that of implementation of the planning. I believe that we must not commit the serious error of underestimating the resources that Christians are able to mobilize for this great effort. In the field of planning we find a flourishing group of institutions located in various countries, the majority of which are carrying out their activities isolated from each other, often concentrated in a single diocese with no serious effort to achieve unification of purpose and distribution of effort at a regional or national level. Most of these efforts are not only unassociated with the governmental planning authority but even resent any such association for fear of identification with an activity that might appear other than strictly ecclesiastical. The resources possessed by our Latin American Church groups, many of them established through the generous efforts of Christians of other continents, should be used for participation in social research and planning on a broad civic basis, contributing to the more effective accomplishment of the national plan.

PRIVATE SECTOR INITIATIVE BEYOND POLITICAL BORDERS   There is another aspect which could engage our Christian initiative, namely, the possibility of orientating regional planning toward an overall solution of the pressing problems that concern more than one country. The most typical example of this kind concerns the region of the Andean Mountains where peasants numbering more than five million live in three different countries possessing basically similar problems.

Our association with national organizations concerned with development planning in no way implies the improper subordination of entities under Church sponsorship to less effectual accomplishment under the state. On the contrary, it is a question of becoming involved in a new front in which Christian action is not only indispensable but will be most efficacious in helping to enlist sectors of Latin American society of top importance for national development.

With reference to the actual implementation of plans through well elaborated projects, we should make certain that identification and recognition as an important part of the national effort are given to current Church activities already operating numerous projects of social development throughout the continent. For example, with regard to education we should call attention to the fact that there are in Latin America about 5,000 private educational institutions prepared to share in current educational programs throughout the continent. The private universities and centers of technical training in the fields of agriculture, labor and cooperatives could double the potential for professional and technical training if they would participate on a national basis in serving the more pressing needs of society.

BROAD HORIZONS FACE LAY PROGRAMS   We must work also in the preservation of the progress which has been achieved in the areas of social welfare now being emphasized (housing, education, public health). Lay groups such as Catholic Action in different spheres—Legion of Mary, St. Vincent de Paul, Caritas—which up to now have directed their efforts mainly towards religion and welfare activities should expand their programs and focus some of their work on projects planned by specialists. This would permit the channelling of their zeal, their organization and their spirit of sacrifice as powerful resources to be put at the disposal of society. Among such works, surely, programs of community improvement will be especially attractive to these lay groups.

Thus the Church might consider putting its knowledge and resources to more effective use in preparing programs and projects for adaptation to national and regional needs. They should select carefully those with the capacity to fulfill so that they may obtain financing from national or international sources to complement their own contributions, thus enlarging the scope of their activities.

SECTION IV

Religio-social Considerations

The Church and Social Revolution in Latin America

Most Rev. Mark G. McGrath, C.S.C.

THE SENSE OF "REVOLUTION" Barbara Ward, widely read Catholic economist, begins her book entitled *The Rich Nations and the Poor Nations* with the flat statement, "I suppose we are all aware of the fact that we live in the most catastrophically revolutionary age that men have ever faced."

Vice-President Hubert Humphrey, who honored this meeting with his presence last year, writes in a recent issue of *Foreign Affairs*, "Although the observation that Latin America is in the midst of a political, economic and social revolution has become a commonplace, it is true."

The influential Chilean magazine, *Mensaje*, published by the Jesuit Fathers, dedicated an entire issue in December of 1962 to the theme, "Revolution in Latin America;" and followed this up with another special issue in October, 1963, on "Revolutionary Reforms in Latin America." Early in 1964 the *Civilta Cattolica*, published in Rome by the Jesuits, carried a critique of these two issues of *Mensaje* by Father Jarlot, which questioned the prudence of using the term "revolution" in a Christian context, pointing out that it is loaded with Marxist overtones. Not only does it signify rapid structural changes, Father Jarlot asserts, but also connotes violence and some measure of hate and class warfare. He would prefer the term "evolution." Mr. Humphrey, in the article already mentioned, asks the question: "Is it appropriate to define Alliance [for Progress] policy as favoring social 'revolution'—or should this word be avoided in favor of 'evolution' or some other expression?" He answers: " 'Evolution', if carefully examined, proves to be inadequate, for it implies an unconscious, non-deliberate change that is slow and gradual. What is required is conscious, rapid change in the socio-economic structure, a process that can correctly and precisely be called a revolution. If used not as a slogan but in its precise sense, the policy of peaceful social and economic revolution is a correct characterization of Alliance policy. We should not hesitate to identify ourselves with it in Latin America, just as President Johnson associated himself with it in his 'war on poverty' throughout the world when he recently remarked: 'If a peaceful revolution in these areas is impossible, a violent revolution is inevitable.' "

TERM "REVOLUTION" IS AMBIGUOUS   We must recognize that the term "revolution" is terribly ambiguous. We speak of the industrial revolution; we may even speak of intellectual, scientific or religious revolutions. Politically the term "revolution" can be used to describe anything from a military coup d'etat, which in effect changes nothing except the man in charge; to a revolution of independence, such as all the American nations have experienced, by which they severed their allegiance to foreign powers while continuing to develop in their familiar ideological and social patterns; or to a communist revolution, such as Cuba now suffers, which violently breaks a people from its ancient ideals and thrusts it into new molds, ideological, economic and political.

The term "revolution" has been so used and abused in Latin America that to a Catholic in Mexico it may be repulsive; to a Catholic in Brazil meaningless; and to a Catholic in Chile necessary. For the one it connotes religious persecution and political oppression; to the second it is merely a political phrase, the common currency of every politician; to the third it is a description, however general, of the longing for fundamental social changes which the great mass of the population ardently and justly desires.

Can the term "revolution" be used in a Christian sense? It depends who uses it and where. The directors of this CICOP meeting have chosen to use the specific term "social revolution" to describe a process which is not only desirable but urgently necessary. Previous speakers on this program have graphically described the changes that are taking place in Latin America. We would like to point out why we cannot simply fear and oppose these changes; but must strive to discover their meaning and give them their direction, without violence, without hate, for the benefit of all. The changes we are experiencing are both quantitative and qualitative. They augment considerably our daily task as Christians; and they diversify it more and more. Not to see this and yet to plunge ahead in a generous effort to save Latin America for God or for democracy as might have been done fifty years ago is to forget that there are now three times as many people in Latin America, most of whom live, think and react quite differently from the customary pattern of fifty years ago.

THE CHURCH AND CHANGE   When we speak of the "Church and Social Revolution in Latin America" we must divide our considerations into two aspects: first, the Church and social change, somewhat in the abstract; and, secondly, the Church amidst the profound and rapid change that now affects Latin American society.

Many have remarked that we Catholics must develop a theology of progressive change. We have in late centuries often allowed ourselves to fall into a mentality of fixity regarding all the aspects of our Christian belief and practice that would freeze forever in equal permanency what is essential and what is transitory in our teaching and in our worship. Take the liturgy for instance. How difficult it was for us to "get over the hump" of resistance to the use of the vernacular in the Mass. Latin in the liturgy, in the minds of most of us, had taken on a permanency and necessity almost equal to the dogma of transubstantiation. Almost up to the eve of the Council those who spoke or wrote in favor of introducing the vernacular into the celebration of the Mass were widely considered thoughtless rebels who were toying with the very deposit of the faith. Yet now, *post factum*, after the publication of the Constitution on the Sacred Liturgy, we recognize that not only the use of Latin but also the employment of many other elements of cult in the Mass (vestments, gestures, Gregorian chant, etc.) are historical accretions, which in their time represented improvements in the manner of dramatizing the divine sacrifice and which may and must be subject to change in our time and in the future, under the careful guidance of Church authority, so that this sacrifice will be more intelligible and meaningful and more fruitfully shared in by the peoples of new centuries and different cultures.

PROGRESS IN DOCTRINE   Even in matters of doctrine we have been taught by the Council to recognize, to expect and even to encourage progressive change. Revealed doctrine, the word of God, the deposit of faith—this does not change. "Though heaven and earth should pass away," said the Lord, "My word will stand" (Mark 13:31). But there has been through the centuries, there is now and there will be until the end of time progress in our increased understanding of that Word. Theology is not a closed science, of which we have only to learn and repeat the well-polished conclusions. It is a continual quest for a better understanding of the Word of God as preserved, handed down and interpreted by the living Church. Witness the progress in our time in the understanding of Scripture, through the controlled application of the many linguistic, archaeological and historical sciences developed since the 19th century which are like so many tools with which to delve ever more profoundly into the fuller and more accurate meaning of the revealed Word and the life of the Apostolic Church, where this Word received its first and most significant external form.

It is perfectly reasonable that in our progressive appreciation of the fuller meaning of revelation, in itself and in its application to the ever new circumstances of human life, that there be varying opinions and interpretations. But only the infallible Church, through its papal or conciliar authority, or its universal teaching and belief, can impose upon us any single interpretation of a revealed doctrine. Until this occurs no school of theological opinion, however numerous its exponents, is tantamount to doctrine. Furthermore, even when a doctrinal interpretation becomes for us an integral part of the doctrine itself, through the infallible teaching of the Church, this does not close down that doctrine nor end our intellectual search and progress in its regard, but generally opens up a whole series of new vistas to be explored for a further and richer understanding. In March of last year, when I enjoyed the privilege of a private audience with the Holy Father, he referred to one notable progress in our understanding of revealed doctrine simply and feelingly. "Is it not marvelous," he said, "that after twenty centuries the Church now comes to define herself!" Truly the progress obtained in our own lifetimes in a theological penetration of the Church's inner life and her meaning for the world is a living testimony of the Holy Spirit active in the progressive enrichment of our Catholic faith. These observations on a dynamic and progressive approach to an understanding of revelation have a bearing, too, on our approach to social change.

SENSE OF HISTORY Many Catholics, wedded to an exaggerated fixity in all matters concerning the teaching and the practice of the Church, unconsciously project this attitude into an opposition towards or at least a suspicion of all change in the social realm. This is ironical in our age of such rapid change in all orders of science, technology and human relations. It is ironical most of all in an age in which the search for a meaning in progress, for the sense and interpretation of history is so fundamental to modern thought. To say that we Catholics require a theology of progressive change means also and perhaps above all that we must acquire once more a theology of history, a dynamic sense of history which is our fundamental birthright and which we have too often and too unconsciously renounced.

It is the biblical revelation, centered in the fact of the resurrection of Christ, which introduced into the world the dynamic and progressive sense of history, of a march forward to a consummate happiness for all which dominates our western world and which has projected the "doctrine of progress" across the entire world. Yet we have often in our own modern centuries retreated to a quiet and static effort to construct our Christian life upon this earth and in our own times, with little or no real reference to what has happened in the past or to the future which our lives and actions must prepare.

INCORPORATION OF ALL MEN INTO DIVINE LIFE   Fortunately for us the modern biblical, patristic and liturgical movements in the Church have once more centered our faith and its theological expression within the context of the history of salvation. Revelation is once more for us, as it is in the Bible and as it was for the early Fathers of the Church, the history of God's dealings with man: from creation to the promised parousia, the return of the Lord, when new heavens and a new earth will consummate the work of God in mankind developed through the centuries of time. The Word of God, made man, who died and rose again that we might rise with him, now from sin and finally into glory, is the key to a Christian sense of history. All of history is now the progressive incorporation of all men into the divine life through Christ who has taken on our nature, washed it of its sin, and thus brought it about that "all who welcomed him, he empowered to become the children of God, all those who believe in his name" (John 1:12). This redemption is not realized in the abstract, but is to be worked out in the conditions of our terrestrial existence and our social living together during the space of time allotted each of us in the progress toward eternity. God, who redeems us through his Word, also created us and all that exists through that same Word—for, says St. John (1:3), "It was through him that all things came into being, and without him came nothing that has come to be." From the beginning, as is so graphically stated in the first chapters of the book of Genesis, man was charged with all of material creation in the name of God: to people the earth and bring it into subjection (Gen 1:28).

Nothing fits more into the biblical concept of things than the tremendous progress which man is making in our times toward a more complete domination of God's creation. "God's glory," said Pascal, "is the glorification of man." This is true within the context of creation. It does not imply an anthropocentric view of life—interpreting God in human terms. It rather means that it is in fact God's revealed will that all the universe be subjected to man, for his glory, for his life, for he is made in the image and likeness of God "in praise of his glory."

CHRISTIAN SENSE OF PROGRESS These are not or should not be merely abstract theological theses. Douglas Hyde has remarked frequently how important it is for the communists to get across to even the most ignorant of those they catechize the marxist sense of history: the necessary struggle of the classes which will inexorably terminate in a classless society of justice and equality for all. If this truncated, materialized version of Christian hope has so successfully stirred to startling heights of sacrifice and devotion indigenous communist leaders in every corner of the globe, how much more the entire message of hope! There is nothing good and holy in the marxist promises which is not better set forth in that Christian attitude toward the world which Second Vatican Council is now studying in its projected Constitution on the Church in the Modern World. We, too, desire and work for an expansion of all material means of production and welfare, so that in our century, for the first time in recorded history, all men may have access to a material standard and an education which will free them from the slavery to bodily want and the sad, almost animal dimness of life without knowledge, without culture, without joy, without beauty, without love.

THE CONTINUING SPIRITUALIZATION OF THE MATERIAL   But in so doing we look beyond material progress to the progress of man. The communists have twisted the message of Genesis about so as to make man the slave of matter once more, under the guise of greater material production for the wants of mankind. The authentic biblical message subjects matter to spirit, and the rest of creation to man and man to God. Christopher Dawson once wrote that all progress consists in the continued spiritualization of the material, and the continued divinization of the spiritual. We do not look upon mankind as a mass, nor merely as so many hands that can work and so many mouths that need to be fed; but as a society, composed of distinct human persons, however innumerable, each of whom loves and is loved by men in the love of God. But to love, man must eat, he must work, he must learn, he must become every day more human, which is to say more spiritual—through his free control of material nature. "Mortal no more, they (men) will be as the angels in heaven," said our Lord, and in a true sense, which requires careful definition, this process of spiritualization must begin upon earth and is a fundamental explanation of our long individual and collective preparation for eternal life.

That there is no necessary relation between greater culture and greater sanctity, is a fact that stares us in the eyes; but that there should be is a principle we must proclaim and which is clearly borne out in the lives of most of the Church's canonized saints.

THE COUNCIL AND CHANGE IN THE MODERN WORLD   Most of what we have said so far is valid not only for Latin America, but also for the entire world in which we live today. It describes, quite fundamentally, the meaning of the Second Vatican Council, as this meaning has gradually unfolded.

Few could have described this meaning five years ago when the Council was announced, nor even two and a half years ago when it began. The bishops assembled in Rome for the first session in October of 1962 found before them an enormous amount of material, in more than seventy drafts of Constitutions, covering almost every conceivable aspect of Church life. Pope John XXIII pointed out clearly in his discourse at the opening Mass that the bishops were not gathered together to repeat old doctrines nor to condemn new errors, but rather to speak a Christian message to the modern world. He spoke of *aggiornamento;* the bringing up to date of the Church's action in a changed world. This was to be a pastoral council. Some took this to mean a non-doctrinal council, a council concerned merely with practical measures easily conceived and easily decreed. But after two months of arduous debate this notion was effectively corrected. If at all times pastoral action must flow from a clear doctrinal understanding of where it is going, it must do so now more than ever. Speaker after speaker described how alien our liturgy had become to our people devoid for so many of doctrinal understanding and personal participation; how alien to them also was the living voice of scripture and tradition, the Word of God; how completely modern thought was dominated by the secularized media of mass communication; how alien to the Church were so many of the dominant factors and forces at work in the construction of a new world civilization, whose day has already begun to dawn.

THE CHURCH TO THE WORLD It was this rising realization which prompted three epochal discourses on the Council floor—delivered by Cardinal Suenens, Cardinal Lercaro and the then Cardinal Montini, now our Holy Father Paul VI—which concurred in centering the attention of the Council upon the Church, firstly considered in herself, and then in her mission in the world. The Council since that moment, has developed upon these two axes, expressed in the two Constitutions on the Church and on the Church in the Modern World, to which, after the introduction to our whole theme through the fruitful discussion of the liturgy, all the other Consititutions and declarations of the Council are related as particular aspects.

This vision did not simply occur in the Council. It crystallized, after generations of concentrated effort, notably introduced by the social encyclicals of Pope Leo XIII, an effort which can be traced through the doctrinal and pastoral guidance of the great modern pontiffs, particularly in their encyclicals through the liturgical and biblical movements, through the attempted renovation of the religious life, the gradual formulation of a social doctrine of the Church for our age, the growing consciousness of the Church, so vitally nurtured in Pope Pius XII's encyclical on the Mystical Body, the driving encouragement by that same Pontiff and his beloved successor for world consciousness among Catholics, in the missions, in aid to Africa, to Latin America, in every form of international action.

All this crystallized in the Council—in the minds and through the words of zealous bishops, who brought to Rome their anguish over the Church in the Congo, in Viet Nam, in Europe, spiritually bruised by the hate of two terrible wars, in the Americas, North and South.

This process has not ended. It began before the Council. It is crystallizing in the Council, which will be our guide, doctrinal and pastoral for generations, perhaps centuries to come. It will continue after the Council, depending on what you and I do to make the Council real. It is taking place here and now, in this second CICOP meeting.

THE CHURCH AND SOCIAL REVOLUTION IN LATIN AMERICA When we discuss the Church and the social revolution in Latin America, we are discussing the Church in the modern world, in that part of the world where one third of her number is to be found, often convulsed and confused by the change which they witness every day. In future years CICOP meetings will undoubtedly go into the more directly religious preoccupation of the Church in Latin America, the consideration of the Church in herself, in her faith and in her worship and in her own mysterious life in God. This year we are discussing the Church in the Latin American temporal order, in her meaning for that world now and for the future.

To do so, it is obvious that we must speak of *aggiornamento,* adaptations, bringing up to date of the Church's action through all her members in Latin America. But it is equally obvious that this must not be a merely pragmatic singling out of facile and immediate solutions. We are called upon to re-think the very nature and mission of the Church, as proclaimed by Christ, lest we unconsciously falsify his purposes; and to re-think the living out of that mission in circumstances so changed and changing. This was obvious to some before the Council; and they were responsible in part, along with their brothers of like mind in Africa, Asia, North America, Europe and the world, under the guiding spirit of the popes, for the clear direction taken by the Council. Now, after three sessions of the Council, it must be obvious to all.

THE CALL FOR SOLID RELIGIOUS THINKING   Our task is to study and effectuate the Church's role in the social revolution now affecting Latin America. How must we go about it?

First of all, we must not close our eyes to the change that is taking place. To do so and to pretend that the Church can carry out its pastoral labors exactly as she has done during the first four centuries of Christianity in this area of the globe is to neglect the very mission of the Church, which is to prolong the teaching and the incarnation of the Word in the different and changing circumstances of time and of place.

Secondly, we must study the facts of change. The theology of history, the history of our salvation, requires an intimate knowledge of the facts of history, both divine and human, the signified will of God and the actual state of mankind. Solid religious thinking about social revolution in Latin America requires a continual dialogue between our theologians and the most competent students of all the human sciences—philosophers and litterateurs, as well as historians, economists, sociologists and political scientists. There are times when nothing can be more harmful to men and to the Church than a doctrinal truth uttered with no reference to the real circumstantial context of the man and the moment; or, what is worse, expressed from a point of view corresponding to an age and a circumstance long gone by.

To this purpose, we must encourage the organization and operation of centers of serious socio-economic research in relation to the circumstances of the life and work of the Church. Many of these centers already exist in Latin America, on the spot, where they must function. These must be built up and more must be founded. They must be financed and staffed with trained personnel, even at the cost of building fewer churches, schools or other institutions. We will do better in all these areas when we see more clearly what we must do. Social research must be intimately related to theological thinking, within and without our faculties and seminaries of theology, to bring the illumination of the Divine Word to bear upon the mission of the Church here and now. This, too, is being done and must be encouraged.

IMPARTING THE VISION TO ALL   This vision of the Church in our modern world must be imparted—to our clergy, to our religious, to our laity, from the pulpit, through congresses, great and small, in the classroom, and in specialized pastoral institutes, such as are now functioning in various nations of Latin America.

The Church through its members must more consciously participate in the living currents of Latin American life, the sources and dynamos of its present revolution: above all the universities, so neglected by us, outside of our few Catholic universities, so intensely cultivated by the communists—

since it is in the universities that the future of Latin America is now being prepared, in thought, and in the formation of those leaders who will be the principal artisans of that future; our Catholic leaders must act in the labor unions, in the agrarian movements, cooperatives and others, in all forms of education, marriage and family orientation, and mass communication, as well as in politics.

Do we mean to say that nothing has been done in these regards? On the contrary, much has been done and is being done; but much more remains to be done. We must not interrupt nor slow down this action, but we must, as the whole Church is doing in the Council, and as Paul VI urges us to do, for instance in his encyclical *Ecclesiam Suam*, take pause to think it out from its foundations and to continue to do so for all the years to come. As Bishop Wright so aptly said, in introducing part of the text of the Constitution on the Church in the Modern World to the Council floor: this text is not the last word, but the first in a new dialogue between the Church and the modern world. Our words in this CICOP meeting are part of this continuing dialogue.

CATHOLIC ATTITUDES TOWARD THE SOCIAL REVOLUTION IN LATIN AMERICA   I have spoken of what we must do to study our situation in a continuing manner. But, clearly, much study and meditation has already been done. What do they show?

First, the rapid emergence of Latin America from feudal and semi-feudal structures, a process comparable to that of Europe, except that what took centuries there is occurring in our lifetimes in Latin America, along with the cultural and value mutations wrought by modern science, technology and mass media of communication, and the tremendous pressure brought to bear by the fervid expansion of our population—all of this has converted poverty into misery for millions upon millions, dismembered society so that there is little sense of security for these and millions more, who no longer belong to the recognizable family or paternalistic hacienda type system of the past. It has created a sense of rising urgency, amidst doubt as to what to do and how. This has been described by other speakers on this program.

What is obvious is that the Church cannot remain passive in face of such a situation of moral and social doubt of so many. She would always have to speak and act, and the more so that the great bulk of the persons caught up in this turmoil are members of the Church. The magisterium must guide the faithful in the many new moral judgments to be made; the faithful must consciously incarnate these values.

The Church in Europe—magisterium and faithful—had to face up to such a crisis. The history of moral theology illustrates the fact that the newer problems of social morality—for example that of usury or the just wage—were sometimes too slowly recognized, sometimes resolved late. The same held for the action of Catholics consequent upon a clearer view of their social obligations. Thus we had, in the words of Pope Pius XI, the scandal of the nineteenth century in Europe, the loss of the working class; and thus we have had, in the words of Pope Paul VI, the tragedy in this century of a Europe that has achieved a great new economic expansion after two tragic wars, but with too little reference to the spiritual values of man and society.

APPLYING SOCIAL DOCTRINE IN LATIN AMERICA   The Church in Latin America faces up to a more rapid and acute crisis of social morality. Where for four centuries morality, the very concept of human relations, was limited to the family type "me and thee" give and take, we must now project our moral sense out over a broad new social complex. The evolving social doctrine of the Church, evolving since Pope Leo XIII, against the background of the European capital and labor strife, for many years sounded foreign to Catholics in Latin America. This is no longer so. We now see that we have the same problems Europe had and others as well.

The primary mission of the Church magisterium at all times is to proclaim the Word of God to all men. In Latin America today, perhaps our greatest urgency is to project that same divine Word and revelation upon a broad social scale. The principal contribution of the Church to change in Latin America is the clarification of the principles of justice and charity which require it and must also guide it. The right and duty of the Church to teach in these areas has been abundantly illustrated by pertinent texts of all the recent popes. It was Pope Pius XII, however, who most clearly brought out that the Church does not teach social morality as though formulated from vague, remote principles through some long, laborious casuistic process. Rather it regards man in his total context—human and divine—and speaks out for the defense of his full human and Christian dignity. It is this regard which makes us favor Christian social revolution in Latin America—toward a situation of fuller human and Christian dignity for all our people.

A CORRECT CONCEPT OF REVOLUTION Once again we turn to the concept of "revolution." The term itself has been pre-opted in this century by the advocates of class warfare, of hate and of violence and subversion. That is why it is probably best for us to speak always not merely of revolution but of Christian revolution, of social revolution or of peaceful revolution.

By so doing we free ourselves of the more obvious cruelties of the marxist method, but also from some more subtle over-simplifications which sometimes can infect our own talk.

We cannot conceive of revolution as a complete change, in the absolute sense. To be effective it must be radical, particularly in the new structures it seeks, but must also carry over many institutions and values from the past which must still serve. Nor should we fall into the facile manner, favorable to the advocates of violence, which would promise "pie-in-the-sky" tomorrow—as though by some quick political blow we could obtain the new structures our society needs without the long patient labor of human formation and economic development which must provide the understructures. This is particularly dangerous in the top heavy power structure of Latin America where the temptation to immediate political action so often tends to short-circuit this work of building the understructures. Nor, theologically, can we fall into the perennial error of the revolutionary who speaks of a perfect world which will never come about on this earth, where, due to human limitation and the reality of sin, man's life upon earth, singly and collectively, will always be what Job described it to be: a never ending "struggle" (Job 7:1).

CHANGE MUST BE WORKED FOR   Granting all the conditions, nonetheless, we realize that the kind of social change we must hope for in Latin America will not merely happen. We must deliberately work for it.

This requires, as we have pointed out, a far more explicit ideology of Christian hope for man on earth, in connection with and tending to his eternal reward, and not fundamentally opposed to it. No longer can we Christians appear as those who simply suffer history and let it happen, while marxists pretend to understand its laws and be its makers. Neither the marxist, who pretends that history proceeds according to determined and inexorable laws, nor the old style economic liberal, who pretends to canonize selfishness by saying that each should work for himself and history would take care of itself: neither of these takes a responsible view of history—within which we progress according to the measure of our sincere and responsible effort for a better world, and according to our measure of man.

No point is dearer to Catholic social teaching than the insistence on the human person, as the center and reason for the progress of things and of society. No amount of economic planning from above can achieve the development of the whole man nor of the truly human society. Father Vekemans has stressed the fact that the masses of our people are now atomized, separated, powerless, subject to the action of the state, which tends to act more and more for them and directly upon them, because they are not formed for action and lack the intermediate organizations of family, community and specialized endeavor which should channel their own free and dynamic work for a better existence. We must grasp the fact that our masses were for centuries tied into a static aristocratic structure which held them in place while it required little of them. It gave them a kind of security, particularly on the hacienda-type rural pattern, but required of them little responsible action.

FORMING MILLIONS TO THE NEW SOCIETY   As this old structure disappears the innumerable millions find themselves isolated on the land, or in the city slums or in the precarious existence of the proletariat. Europe, also, grew out of feudal structures into democracy. This process took centuries and is not yet complete. In Latin America we are trying to do it in one generation. Democracy, if it is to be government not only for the people but also of and by them, requires responsible citizens. We do not create democracy by merely giving the right to vote to all citizens. Our great passive masses, never used to thinking or acting for themselves, will often either sell their vote to the rich or cast it with the demagogue. Our great passive masses will too typically expect everything to be done for them, either by the State or by the popular leader or by the Church. We have before us a tremendous task not merely of education but of formation, not merely in schools but in learning to work together consciously toward goals of progress within liberty, the task of helping the passive masses to become responsible individual citizens. We face this task in the religious order, wherein our Catholics' commitment will be less and less the result of structures which maintain the faith, and more and more the result of personal choice. We face the same task in the temporal order. The two orders are closely intertwined.

Thus it is that the intense desire for personal responsibility and intermediate structures flows from the Christian vision of man. Thus it is that the Catholic should favor every local effort which draws individuals into communal action, forming them in a consciousness of the dignity and respon-

sibility of each. Thus it is that we insist that reform programs, whether national or Alliance for Progress, should
avoid the pitfall of promoting ever more omnipotent states,
which may arrive at the immediate care of material needs
but will never form the responsible, free and active citizens
that democracy requires. Every Christian social promotion
must respect these values.

THE CHURCH'S GRAVE RESPONSIBILITY   But how much is the
Church supposed to promote in the social or temporal order?
Obviously, we must distinguish. Christian Catholics make
up the bulk of the population of Latin America; and consequently bear the major responsibility for its social development. The Church, as an institution, as magisterium, or to
speak simply, the hierarchy of the Church, has the basic
responsibility of preaching the word of God, not only in
its individual but also in its social dimension. This we
have already stressed. Should the Church as an institution
also directly promote programs of economic and social
betterment?

We often say that this should be done whenever other
private and public forces are lacking for the task. This is a
common situation in Latin America. Given the lack of intermediate structures in our midst, in many areas the only
other force at work, apart from the Church, is the government, often too distant, too bureaucratic or too steeped in
political complications. Often, too, the very programs of the
government fail because of the suspicion or passivity of the
people. In many, many instances unless the bishop or the
parish priest or local Catholic groups give moral support to
a program it will not be done; often, too, if they do not
directly promote it, it will not be done.

When the Church, as an institution, fills in for the lack of
intermediate structures, it retires from the area when these
structures have been created. This is the ideal; and there
are many examples where this has already been done.

But besides filling in for others the Church must fill out

to their full human and spiritual dimension so many efforts in the socio-economic sphere. The insistence on the formation of the persons involved for their social responsibility is a case in point. There are many others. A merely technical approach to the problem of development, lacking in the ideology of human values, is a dangerous thing, convertible to any totalitarian purpose.

CONCLUSION: BROTHERHOOD ON TRIAL Pope Paul VI in his 1964 Christmas message stated: "Democracy, to which all mankind appeals today, must take on a more universal aspect which will transcend all the obstacles in the way of effective brotherhood among men."

Effective brotherhood is on trial in the world, in the developed nations of the world which have not yet found the heart for the kind of massive commitment needed to help their brother nations through their crises to that minimum condition of economic freedom which will make political freedom more meaningful. Effective brotherhood is on trial in Latin America, where free, expanding democracy is often only beginning to be a reality. Vice-President Humphrey, speaking last year in the Senate, insisted that in the revolutionary atmosphere prevalent in much of Latin America "ideological factors are often as important as straight economic programs." (March 21, 1964) There is no substitute for the Church, in its hierarchy and in all its members, as the principal source of this ideological strength in Latin America today. This has been the burden of my address.

What I have said is information brought to this CICOP meeting. But it is not the whole meaning of CICOP, which is as broad as the Church herself. We here assembled, cardinals, archbishops, bishops, priests, religious, lay persons of many and quite diverse backgrounds and occupations: we are the Church. If effective brotherhood is on trial within each of our nations, and between our nations; it is above all we Christians, disciples of Him whose principal commandment is love for our brother, who must give leadership in bringing our nations and our world successfully through the trial.

In our own times we are witnessing the struggle of Christianity in Africa and Asia to disassociate itself from the old colonial policies of the European nations. Christianity in many areas of the East has been coldly rebuffed because of this association.

CHRISTIANITY IN OUR HEMISPHERE   Christianity is also on trial in our hemisphere. The challenge is seen differently by North Americans than by Latin Americans; but it is the same challenge: to find the sense of our times in effective brotherhood. This is the fundamental social revolution we must bring to our times.

In this spirit we can work with all men, as Pope John XXIII points out in concluding his encyclical, *Pacem in Terris*. "There lies ahead," he says, "an immense task for all men of good will, if the mutual relations of the human family are to be restored in truth, in justice, in love and in freedom. This is a most exalted task, for it is a task of bringing about true peace in the order established by God—an order founded on truth, built according to justice, vivified and integrated by charity, and put into practice in freedom."

CHAPTER 12

The Bright Light of Progress

Juan Cardinal Landázuri Ricketts

I want to present a factual picture, simply and candidly, of certain aspects of the Catholic Church today in Latin America. I shall divide my remarks into four main points: the first point will be the progress the Catholic Church has made in Latin America in recent years; second, some of the major problems the Church currently faces in Latin America; third, the recent help sent by North American Catholics to the Church in Latin America; fourth, a few guidelines for the kind of help Latin America still requires.

First of all, I wish to make it clear that I do not pretend to be a spokesman for all of Latin America. I am only one bishop out of hundreds. As the Archbishop of Lima, I find myself shepherd of one of the oldest dioceses in the New World, the former capital of the Spanish Empire in South America, a diocese founded sixty years before the Pilgrims landed on Plymouth Rock, a city which glories in four canonized saints.

While Lima may be typical of Latin America in some respects, in others it is quite distinct. Let us remember: Latin America is a vast area, and although we can speak in general terms of problems and needs of the total region, still, the individual differences of the various countries are marked. We must realize, for instance, that several languages are spoken in Latin America. We speak Portuguese in Brazil, French in Haiti, Quechua in the Andes mountains, and Spanish just about everywhere else. Also, governments and economies, geography and communications vary considerably.

Because such social, political and climatic differences affect the Church, I think it is necessary to remind ourselves from time to time that it can be quite misleading to generalize too much about a reigon in which live 200 million people of various cultural, linguistic and racial backgrounds.

THE PROUD FACT OF PROGRESS   Regarding the four points I mentioned, the first point at issue concerns the progress which the Church in Latin America has achieved in recent years, especially since World War II when, among other significant events, hundreds of displaced missioners from the Orient were shifted to Latin America.

Following the publication of Father John J. Considine's famous book, *Call for Forty Thousand*, literally thousands of missioners from all parts of the world poured into Latin America; and in the last few years the pace has even quickened due to the urgent pleas of the beloved Pope John XXIII, and of the gloriously reigning Pope Paul VI. From Spain alone there are now eighteen thousand missioners in Latin America. United States missioners now number more than four thousand.

In 1945, there were 23,300 priests in all of Latin America. In 1960, there were 37,500—an increase of more than 50% in 15 years. In the last four years, the number of priests in Peru, for example, has increased 22%, while the population of the country has advanced only 20%.

The chief contribution missioners from abroad make in Latin America is not to fill-in for missing clergy. They do this, of course, and they do it well. But more important, they bring with them new ideas, new approaches, new enthusiasm and a new zeal.

The work of Father Roger Vekemans in Chile is a case in point. As director of DESAL, Father Vekemans has contributed substantially to Chile's advanced socio-economic program in which the Church plays so effective a role.

In Bolivia, Ecuador and Peru, Father Thomas Verhoeven has organized a system for training volunteer catechists which has already prepared more than 3,000 teachers in the far reaches of the Andes Mountains.

Most of you are familiar with the work of Father Daniel McLellan, who has revolutionized private credit in a half dozen countries in Latin America, through the parish credit cooperative.

ABLE LATIN AMERICAN LEADERS   While foreign missioners have been doing outstanding work, native-born priests have not been lacking in productive activity. The splendid apostolate of Monsignor Joaquin Salcedo, who has organized a vast network of radio schools to reach thousands of rural people in Colombia, is spreading rapidly to many other countries.

Bishop Alonso Escalante of Mexico has founded the first foreign mission society in Latin America, and already has several priests in Japan and over 200 Mexican seminarians.

Latin America is very proud of its vigorous Christian Family Movement (CFM), so ably promoted by Argentina's Father Pedro Richards. The Legion of Mary and the Cursillos de Cristiandad have been planted and are thriving in most Latin American countries. The same is true of Serra International, an organization aimed at developing vocations.

New seminaries are rising all over Latin America. Peru, for example, opened ten new seminaries in the last five years. These seminaries are modern in every respect, with academic programs approved by secular educational authorities, and faculties selected from various countries around the world.

STRIKING PROGRESS IN EDUCATION   It is in the field of education that the Church has made some of her most striking progress, and on all levels. Catholic schools in Chile are supported in great part by the government and most parishes have some kind of school. Fifteen years ago there were no parish schools in Peru, but now there are several dozen; three years ago there was only one Catholic college or university, and now there are five.

One of the most important features of the Church's advance in Latin America in recent years is the changing image of the Church in the eyes of the general public. In recent years the hierarchies in Latin America have taken an aggressive stand on the urgency of social and economic reform, with strong public declarations. The bishops of Brazil, Chile, Colombia, Bolivia and Peru, to mention a few, have sharply defined the need for reform. Three years ago, in Lima, I prepared and ordered to be preached in all the parishes of the Archdiocese a series of 22 sermons on social justice. I know that the contents were effective because the series had hardly begun, when pressure built up to cancel them. I am pleased to say that the sermons continued, and I know that they were a source of encouragement for the poor and a source of guidance for those in positions of power and policy.

Even on the material plane, the Church in Latin America is growing stronger. More and more of our people are beginning to realize that government support for the Church is uncertain and insignificant at best, and that consequently they themselves must contribute.

The sacramental life of the people strengthens from day to day. All over Latin America the people are fulfilling their Sunday obligation and the Easter Duty with more exactitude, and it is particularly noticeable that men are going to church more regularly.

NO ROOM FOR COMPLACENCY   However, this optimistic exposition of some of the recent progress of the Church in Latin America should not lull us into a fatal complacency. The problems that we still face are monumental. It would be very easy to recite a litany of the Church's problems, but I would prefer to assemble them under two general headings: first, the enormous religious ignorance of the great masses of people; second, the appalling shortage of vocations to the priesthood and the religious life.

It is not uniquely Latin American phenomena, but it is true that in many parts of Latin America the religion of the people is divorced from their everyday lives. Almost everyone is baptized a Catholic, but few comprehend what the profession of their faith implies. In some regions, more than half of the children are canonically illegitimate, because less than half of the couples are married by the Church. This obviously cuts drastically into the sacramental life of the people.

In large areas of Latin America, the Church has only a slight influence on the education of youth. In many countries the Catholic religion is taught, by law, as part of the curriculum in the public schools. However it not infrequently happens that the religious classes are taught by professors who know little about the subject themselves, or, who are even enemies of all religion. The situation is particularly serious in many of the institutions of higher learning where enemies of the Church control the preparation of teachers, of lawyers, of doctors and of future leaders.

IGNORANCE IS NOT FROM BAD WILL But doctrinal ignorance and consequent lack of religious practice do not come, in general, from bad will. It is clear that enemies of the Church are active, but the vast majority of the people are people of good will, who want to do what is right. Time and time again, it is the laymen who edify the clergy and who demand more and better spiritual attention. But we just do not have the priests, Brothers, Sisters and lay apostles to assist them.

Consider Honduras, for instance, with only one priest for every 12,500 Catholics! Brazil, the largest Catholic country in the world with 77 million Catholics, has one priest for every 6,400 Catholics. Despite the fact that Peru has received considerable help in recent years, it still has only one priest for every 5,800 Catholics, placing it third after Brazil and Venezuela in terms of shortage of priests in the entire continent. These figures become much more meaningful when we consider that in the United States there is one priest for every 680 Catholics.

A critical lack of vocations, then, is the second of the two

general problems which the Church confronts in Latin
America. The fact is that we are faced with the task of trying to develop vocations today in a continent which has a
very high illiteracy rate, a very high percentage of broken
homes, and very poor religious education.

The poverty and isolation in which many of our priests
live is another cause of the scarcity of vocations. Parents simply do not want their sons to live the way that they have
seen many of the local priests living. Since the masses of the
people are poor in Latin America, the Church too is poor,
and a vocation to the religious life requires more heroism
perhaps, than in many other parts of the globe.

THE NORTH AMERICAN CONTRIBUTION We turn now to the
third point, the contribution of North American Catholics
to Latin America in recent years. Actually, this is perhaps
the most difficult point to discuss, because I do not know
where to begin. Help from the United States and Canada
has been so generous, so widespread, so effective, that one
hesitates to mention any single portion of it, knowing that
it is impossible to mention all.

There are now more than 4,100 North American missioners working in Latin America; these include bishops, priests,
Brothers, Sisters and lay apostles. The Maryknoll Fathers
alone have almost 300 priests in Latin America. Chicago is
well represented in Peru with the Chicago Carmelites and
the Augustinians, as well as several diocesan clergy working
in Panama and Bolivia.

I cannot list here the 49 North American dioceses, the
102 religious communities and provinces of men, or the 161
communities and provinces of women, which have sent
religious personnel to Latin America, or the sixty-four (64)
dioceses which have sent Papal Volunteers. However, I
must not forego the opportunity to thank from the bottom of
my heart a man whose name is a household word in many
parts of Latin Amreica because of his magnificent leadership, his open-hearted generosity, his apostolic vision, his

tireless zeal and Christian love toward the Church in Latin America. I know that I can speak for all Latin America when I express my profound gratitude to Richard Cardinal Cushing, Archbishop of Boston.

C.R.S. SERVES 8,000,000 DESTITUTE   That magnificent creation of the United States hierarchy, Catholic Relief Services, is the difference between life and death for tens of thousands of Latin Americans. Not only in times of disaster from flood and earthquake, but in the daily struggle for existence, Catholic Relief Services provides the needed help to eight million destitute Latins.

Parenthetically, I might remark apropos of Catholic Relief Services, that many bishops in Latin America, as well as many missioners, feel that a change should be made in Public Law Number 480, Title 3, to permit some small charge to be levied on food distributed by welfare groups. The cost of administering the food program is prohibitive for many organizations and the result is that often no food is made available for people who need it most. Secondly, the current system of giving food free to people who could pay a little for it is the best way to destroy whatever ambition and self-esteem those underprivileged people might still possess. In this respect, the recent Christmas address of the Holy Father comes to mind in which he underlined the need for "bread with dignity."

Returning to the theme of North American aid to Latin America, I can say with complete sincerity that in Peru, for instance, there is no missioner more loved than the North American missioner. Time and again I am approached by people who want a new parish, by government officials who want teachers or nurses for schools and hospitals, by bishops who want more priests, Brothers, Sisters and lay apostles, and I tell you frankly that most often they ask me specifically to try and find North Americans. What more can I say?

We now turn to the fourth and final point, a few guidelines for the kind of help that the Church in Latin America still requires. I will treat this briefly under three topics: attitude, personnel, and material resources.

BETTER CONTACTS FOR WARMER FRIENDSHIP In regards to attitude, it is unquestionable that increased contacts between us will clarify the thinking of both North and South Americans. The conditions obtaining in Latin America are the product of forces at work for four centuries and we cannot hope to reverse them substantially in four years, or even one generation. But the more we interchange ideas, plans and opinions, the more we just get to know each other—the more we will be able to help each other. Latin Americans are no more sensitive than any other human beings. We are brothers and sisters to the rest of the world, no more, no less.

Concerning the need for personnel, we require all kinds and as many as possible. I do not deny that other things being equal, the more highly trained personnel will achieve more, but our needs are so vast that there is a place for virtually everyone who is will-intentioned and who possesses normal ability. In general I would urge you to choose missions on the basis of relative need, as shown by statistics; on the basis of the influence you feel that the mission will exert in a given region; and on the basis of the capacity of your own diocese or congregation to fulfill the conditions which the mission would demand.

Neither are there any hard and fast rules for the type of work to accept in Latin America. We need missioners both in the large cities and in the country areas. We need missioners to help mold the conscience of the wealthy, and we need missioners to help enrich the lives of the poor. The tendency today is to enter more and more into the socio-economic field of mission endeavor. I regard the socio-economic apostolate as one of the most important apostolates, especially in our times and particularly in Latin America. But the traditional apostolates of the Church in the fields of teaching, care of the sick, and the deepening of the sacramental life in the parish, must not be abandoned or weakened at any cost.

A PLEA FOR LOW-COST CREDIT Regarding future material assistance, perhaps the greatest requirement that the bishops of Latin America have at the moment is a source of good and inexpensive credit. The governments in Latin America are obtaining such credit from many international financial institutions, but the Church has no such credit source. To build a school for the poor or a new parish in a slum district, or for any other kind of large capital outlay, a bishop must pay fifteen or twenty percent interest to borrow the money locally. One of the most helpful things the North American Catholics could do for the Church in Latin America would be to devise a program for reasonable credit. The Church is the Mother of the poor and will always strive to meet directly the needs of the poor, but in Latin America it is of extreme importance to aid programs that will help the people help themselves, even though the results might not be seen within this generation.

This, then, draws to a close the brief four-point analysis of the Church in Latin America today: her progress, her problems, North American aid and her future needs. During the past two thousand years the Church of Christ has survived many crises more violent than that which now confronts her in Latin America. But perhaps never before has there been so much at stake. Our 200 million Catholics represent one third of the Catholicism of the world, and by the year two thousand demographers predict that our population will triple. This means that Latin America's 600 million population could represent fifty percent of the world's Catholics.

A CONFIDENT TOMORROW If we can continue the advance that is already underway in Latin America, the Catholic Church of the future will be strong indeed. And in my heart I am confident that Church historians of the twenty-first century will write that, despite long years of already generous giving, and despite a multitude of problems at home, the North American hierarchy played a decisive role in the rebirth of the Church in Latin America. They will praise the imagination, the drive, the generosity, the capacity for sacrifice and the fraternal charity that have marked North American missioners, men and women, wherever they are found in this world.

CHAPTER 13

Latin America's Bishops — Our Bond To Their Burdens

Joseph Cardinal Ritter

There are some who can see Latin America rejecting entirely her Christian past to embrace new structures, perhaps communistic in form, or perhaps godless and amoral in some other way. However, it is my studied judgment that this will not be the final eventuality, for there are already many signs that the tide is really turning in favor of Christ and the Church, which is to say that the tide is really turning in favor of Latin America's peoples. Further, we can be absolutely sure that what happens in the Latin America of the future will depend significantly on the Church there and here; that is to say, it depends greatly on those whom we represent, all of us alike chosen by our Lord to be his workers in the world of the present.

THE TIDE IS TURNING   Permit me to offer a number of thoughts as to why it seems to me that the tide is turning and will turn more in favor of the preservation and future flowering of Latin American Catholicism. In the first place, a reason can be found in the wonderful changes and new insights that are being experienced throughout the universal Church in our times, changes and insights which show promise of being far more than a passing vogue. Certainly these following thought trends are rooted in fundamental Christian philosophy and theology.

Recognition of the unity, the equality, the dignity and the

nobility of the human Christian obligation. Recognition of cultures other than our own, such as that of Latin America, despite physical handicaps it may suffer through political and economic weakness, is appreciated as a matter of elementary intelligence.

The Second Vatican Council has given great impetus to the kind of thinking and action so sorely needed by those who wish their helping efforts to go beyond mere good wishes and gestures. For us who are the bishops of the Church, our collegiality involves each of us at the national level in a joint responsibility with each other for the proclamation of the mind of Christ on the subject of regard for the human person and assistance to those in need. In union with the Holy Father, the Apostolic College as never before understands how it is responsible in a collective way for the welfare and growth of the whole Church on a world scale, in the same way that the individual bishop is responsible for the diocese to which he has been assigned.

A STRONG PARISH FOR A STRONG WORLD   For this theory to become effective in practice, each of us who are bishops must recognize that our responsibility is involved in the direction of those members of the clergy who are our co-laborers in the Lord. The three major structural entities in the world Church are the parish, the diocese and the Holy See. Of these three, the parish is by far the most important so far as reaching and teaching the faithful is concerned. The basic working unit of the Church is certainly the parish, to which often in the United States the parochial school is attached. It is the local community of families from which will come the homeland heralds of the Gospel, Christian leadership in public affairs, as well as the vocations for the foreign mission fields.

In order for our people to rise up as a body and labor for the world apostolate, they must be informed on the world apostolate and inspired to participate in it. This ideological formation cannot take place for the mass of our Catholic people at the national or regional level; rather it has to take place at the neighborhood or parish level, and even indeed in great part at the family level. This is why as a bishop I must see that the message through our pastors reaches this level. People must be trained from childhood to understand that devotion to the world apostolate, dedication to genuine respect and concern for all men regardless of their race, color or creed is a foundation stone of all Christian life.

It seems to me today that a bishop must constantly remind himself that simple appeals to individuals will not secure results. There must exist a formulated directing force, educational in nature, clearly accepting its mission in and from the Church, fired with zeal for this mission, working through proper authority, possessed of a carefully designed program, reaching down to the local community level, the parish.

RESPONSIBILITY FOR THE UNIVERSAL APOSTOLATE Frankly, it seems to me that no adequate institution exists as yet in the Church today specifically responsible for the advocacy of the Church's universal pastoral program. The average parish does not possess a clear-cut plan of life and teaching which points the way for participation in the world apostolate, which specifies the implementation of this world apostolate as a fundamental Christian duty. Let us confess it, most of us bishops find ourselves quite ready to permit our many zealous pastors today to lead their flock in some form of participation in the world apostolate as a *work of supererogation*—as a program that is praiseworthy but not at all obligatory.

Very few of us are insistent enough with our people that it is their essential duty as Christians to occupy themselves actively with both the human and the spiritual needs of the peoples of Africa and Asia. Very few of us in years gone by have brought up our people to be actively devoted to the welfare of the Christian millions living as Protestants, either near at hand or at a distance. Very few, again, until very recent days, have taught it as an essential duty for Catholics to concern themselves with the unserved Catholic millions in great areas of Latin America, living without priests and often under sub-human social and economic circumstances.

Let us hope that as a feature in the world-wide *aggiorna-mento* that is with ever-increasing effectiveness taking form through the Ecumenical Council, we bishops, our splendid clergy and devoted Brotherhoods and Sisterhoods, our millions of marvelous faithful will become much more keenly alive to our duties toward our fellow men wherever there is need in the world.

TOWARD MUTUAL RESPECT AND UNDERSTANDING   With regard to Latin America, the task of assisting the Church there to revitalize itself is so enormous that those who want to help must themselves have certain basic attitudes. At the outset is the avoidance of any semblance of paternalism, smugness and insensitivity of the feelings of our Latin American brothers and sisters in Christ. In a book written by several Chilean priests entitled *Land of Hope and Anguish*, there is a chapter called "Santiago is a Long Way from Chicago," in which you will find the passage:

> Our religious workers from North America who labor in Latin America must carry on their tasks in closest possible fraternal harmony with the religious forces of Latin America. They must take pains to acquire a sincere esteem for and full comprehension of the achievements already realized by the Church in Latin America. They must make it a basic principle to seek the cooperation of the Latin American clergy and to seek directives of them. They must take into account the fact that the Church in both our worlds possesses in common a rich religious and spiritual heritage, and that the differences which one notes between our religious practices are almost exclusively external and have their origin not in religious differences but in the diversity of our cultural milieux.

Sound advice for any individual or group that wants to help the Latin American Church.

A second basic attitude is that any assistance rendered

the Church south of our own borders is merely paying a tremendous debt that is ours. The Church in North America was immensely assisted in becoming what it is today by the charity and apostolic spirit of the Church in Europe. Now, thanks to God's goodness, the Church here is of sufficient maturity to exercise this same charity to the Churches south of our national borders. The contribution that is ours to make will be an effort to assist not merely in the development of the organizational Church, but in the creation of a genuine spiritual family, alive, dynamic, loving, self-sacrificial:

A COMMUNITY OF PEOPLE IN CHRIST The goal will not be merely to build church buildings, but to build the Church, a community of people in Christ, the lack of which thousands of houses of worship, schools, and hospitals will not fill. Our goals will include the formation of saintly people and not merely individual saints, a people committed to Christ and Christian service and not merely well-informed people, consciences that speak socially and not merely individually. The kind of formal worship we wish to teach must be concerned not only with statistics about Mass attendance, First Communions, frequency of communion and confession, but with Mass and the Sacraments insofar as they are vitally live encounters with the living, glorious and risen Christ. Lofty ideals, admittedly needed here at home as well as in Latin America, but how else can Christians be formed who will penetrate Latin American society, how else to project the faith and not merely protect it?

And now I would like to become more specific by speaking of a form of assistance between ourselves and Latin America which will bind us together for all the future to come in bonds that are truly Christ-centered and Christ-like. It is a form of aid that has already involved spontaneously nearly half a hundred United States bishops, and which has a potential only beginning to be realized. It is the sending of members of our own diocesan clergy to give a brotherly assist to their fellow priests in Latin America.

OUR BISHOPS CONTRIBUTE THEIR PRIESTS   As of January the first of this year, the bishops of the United States had a total of 179 diocesan clergy at work in Latin America, of whom by far the greatest single group, 74, is under the sponsorship of Cardinal Cushing's Society of St. James the Apostle. In all, and in various ways, 48 dioceses have sent priests, seven of them more than five priests each. Their principal function—almost to be taken for granted—is the operation of parishes; 59 parishes are under their care in 11 different countries. On no previous occasion in the history of the Church in the United States have so many bishops on their own initiative undertaken to place such a substantial number of their diocesan personnel at the disposal of bishops in other nations to meet a crisis.

Since priests from the Archdiocese of St. Louis have been among the number of those serving in Latin America for some time now, I would like to offer the following observations not only for your information but also in the hope that other United States bishops might be prompted to involve their dioceses and clergy in Latin American work. In the first place, this diocesan initiative gives a bishop and the clergy a new mode of apostolic involvement. Funds are constantly being requested for missionary and relief enterprises, and of course that is most necessary, but a new dimension is added when the giving of personnel accompanies our contribution of financial assistance.

Secondly, this initiative has given every member of the diocesan clergy of the Archdiocese of St. Louis a new awareness of the world dimensions of their priestly vocation. When volunteers were sought to leave for Bolivia, the younger clergy responded almost to a man. Every priest I have sent has gone voluntarily after having distinguished himself for priestliness, zeal and initiative here at home; each of the ten I have sent has found a fulfillment and satisfaction so evident that I am completely assured of their love for their work, for Latin America and its people. They have established the finest of relations with the priests of Bolivia, the country of our greatest experience, and on their home visits, have communicated to their brother priests back in their Archdiocese of St. Louis an enthusiasm for the project that assures its continued support.

WARM ENTHUSIASM AMONG THE LAITY   As a third point, I am convinced for a number of reasons that the enthusiasm of the clergy for the project has communicated itself to the laity as well. The laity's response toward the support of the project has been truly heart-warming, and has been accomplished without in any way detracting from what the Archdiocese has been doing for the Church Universal through the Pontifical Mission-Aid Societies, and without the alienation of the Missionary Plan of Cooperation away from its goal of assistance to the Mission-sending Societies of the Church. Quite to the contrary, the gradual growth of all St. Louis mission-aid projects gives credibility to the thesis that Apostolic activity is so interdependent that various Apostolic projects always help and foster one another, when there is careful guidance and supervision. The clergy's enthusiasm for this involvement in Latin America is also measurably responsible for the numerous responses of the laity themselves to the call to become Papal Volunteers.

ST. LOUIS PLEDGES ITS TITHE   Some years ago, through the Pontifical Commission for Latin America, the Holy See extended an urgent invitation to the religious communities of priests, Brothers and Sisters of the United States that within the period of ten years, each religious family make ten percent of its total personnel available for service to the Church in Latin America. If this tithing of consecrated flesh and blood is being asked of and actually being received from our orders and communities, could not a like sacrificial sharing be not also expected with propriety from our dioceses as well? Accordingly, I would like this evening to pledge the Archdiocese of St. Louis to the attainment of this goal, namely, that by the year 1975, with God's assistance, ten percent of our diocesan clergy will be in pastoral service in Latin America, and I confidently express the hope that other dioceses will see fit to set similar goals for themselves.

So that this might be realized with maximum effectiveness, there is need for an overall plan for the recruitment, support and careful placement of this priestly manpower, but this should be well within the competence of the Welfare Conference's Latin America Bureau. For this goal to be really possible, there will be a need for a review of our diocesan structures and present use of priestly personnel, but surely this would be a healthy thing for the Church in our own land.

CHAPTER 14

Private Education in Latin America

Rev. Gustavo Pérez and Rev. Isaac Th. J. Wust

In this paper we intend to present some main trends in Latin American education today in order to suggest an approach that the private sector might take to form an intelligent policy that will correspond to the challenges and needs of Latin America. We hope that these observations will serve as guidelines for those from abroad who are interested in cooperating in the educational development of Latin America.

Before we begin we want to make clear that we do not intend to give a detailed and statistical description of the present situation of education in Latin America either in private or public sectors. This is not yet possible due to a lack of sufficient and accurate data. A recent experience at the first seminar for planning of Catholic education in Latin America held in Melgar, Colombia, with well-known educational experts revealed this clearly. We wanted to spend the first day of the six-day conference discussing the actual situation of Latin America from collected data. After the first long and somewhat heated discussion one of the experts stood up and said that such procedure was counterproductive because at this kind of meeting no one would be able to agree on the statistical facts because no complete studies were available.

Therefore, we intend to sketch in broad outlines the panorama of Latin American education with some suggestions for possible approaches that the private sector might take to assist in its rapid development.

THE NEED OF EDUCATION FOR DEVELOPMENT   First, we would like to clarify a semantic problem so that we will be speaking the same language when we talk about education in general and private education in particular. Education in general, in terms of needs, does not mean the same thing in the United States as it does in Latin America. For the U.S. you have a highly developed society with an integrated, highly organized educational system. Although even in the United States you are in a process of social change, you do not need reforms in your social structure or in your educational system as rapidly as we do in Latin America. We need more than a development of education; we need education for development, as was stated in 1963 by the Brazilian Minister of Education, Paulo de Tarzo Santos. Too much of our educational system in Latin America has been, up to the present, a copy of what was thought to be the ideal in the highly developed countries. For example, in Colombia. The Institute for Agrarian Reform needed topographs for simple measurements. But it was found that graduates with five or six years of university training were unable to do the job because all they had was theory with no practical experience. Now, the Institute trains, in six months, people with only secondary education to do exactly what is needed.

TRAINING PROGRAMS FOR RURAL AREAS   In almost all Latin American countries there are a number of well trained physicians and nurses in the large cities, but what is needed now are new, short training programs for the rural areas where there is practically no medical care at all. Thinking along these lines we might put a question mark on the large number of general declarations that persistently state that what should be done in Latin America is only to eliminate illiteracy. What will we do, if we do teach everyone to read and write in five or ten years, with 40 or 50 million young people if there is no means of integrating them into an adequate economic system that provides employment? In other words, Latin America's educational system should be adapted to the concrete needs of today within a framework of future development.

Secondly, we ought to mention the increased role of governmental and inter-governmental agencies in overall planning activity. Historically, the development of education has been the result of private initiative. But this has changed greatly over the last ten years, especially since 1958 when Gabriel Betancur, former Minister of Education of Colombia and now Assistant General Director of UNESCO, presented a program of overall educational planning to the first meeting of Ministers of Education of the Organization of American States in Lima. One of the reasons was that education became a question of the "to be or not to be" of the whole continent. So the fact that more and more educational responsibilities go to the state as the executive organism of the people is quite a natural process.

HEAVY ROLE OF THE PRIVATE SECTOR But—and we want to stress this emphatically—this does not mean that the private sector can stop or diminish its activities in the educational field. On the contrary, generally speaking, we can say that there will not be educational development as rapid as Latin America needs without an extraordinary effort on the part of the private sector in whatever field we consider: economics, politics as well as education. There are many arguments for this: lack of politico-administrative structure, lack of clear orientation as to where development should go and the lack of funds, even when we take into account the international funds available for this purpose.

We can derive another argument for the importance of the private sector from the following example. In many places people are reluctant to send their children to school because they lack motivation. A father of six boys told me: I have taught five of my sons to farm, why should I send the sixth one to school? It is not only a question of not having any money to pay for classes nor even of not enjoying the income from the child's work, but primarily it is a lack of understanding that going to school means improvement. Therefore educational development should be based on community development techniques in which the private sector can do much to provide the all important element of correct motivation. If the community recognizes and feels a real need for education, they will surely put their efforts into paying, at least partially, for building an adequate educational system.

IMPORTANCE OF IDEOLOGY FOR EDUCATIONAL DEVELOPMENT
On the question of lack of orientation as to where development of education is headed we would like to call your attention to the importance of ideology in the whole development movement. There is a true social revolution going on in Latin America, as you know from the theme of this conference. And since there cannot be revolution without an ideal that moves the people toward drastic action, the element of ideology has become a very important factor. Other papers will clarify this in more detail. In education, we observe that in many countries there is a clear ideological discrepancy not only between various private agencies, but even between the public and private sector. This is especially true in the policy of many convinced and practicing Catholics who insist on having a confessionally established school system excluding cooperation with the public schools, because they do not provide, as they say, a Christian milieu.

They forget that the majority percentage of the baptized Catholic youth attends these public schools. For nearly all at the university level this attitude creates a serious problem. How many cases can we find of excellent and well prepared Christians, including priests and religious men and women, who have been dissuaded from teaching or taking courses in a state university because of so-called leftist tendencies of these universities? This only helps to aggravate the antagonism between Catholic and state universities and, what is worse, these Christian leaders by vocation are forced to abandon the Catholics who make up the large majority of students in Latin American universities in the most formative years of their lives. Furthermore, most of these Catholics must go to state universities for economic reasons and there they are abandoned by Catholic teachers.

In relationship to education for development, there is a trend toward more emphasis on technical and agricultural training since general education has been overemphasized too much in the past. A Brazilian sociologist once said that the surplus of lawyers in Latin America was one of the reasons for underdevelopment. But still, today, too many students take up this career because it gives easy access to political positions. But development depends heavily upon the mechanization of agriculture and industrialization in general. Agrarian reform programs conceived as mere land distribution without corresponding educational programs in agriculture are worthless.

EDUCATIONAL FACILITIES FOR ALL   Finally, a main trend in Latin American education is its socialization effect; the extension of educational facilities to all social classes. The private sector in education has mainly worked with the upper and upper-middle classes in the past since it was easy to finance schools for wealthy families. Although there has been some change over the last few years it is still a general phenomenon that private education serves economically well-off people and the public sector serves those from the lower social strata. A North American priest, a director of an upper class school in a very poor country, told me: "But somebody has to take care of these rich people." When I reminded him that this system creates a division between the private and the public sector and prolongs the gap between the social classes, he answered that he had never thought of it that way. This indicates what I consider a general attitude: that nonparticipation or insufficient participation of the private sector in the movement toward integration of the social classes into a harmonious social structure is not due so much to unwillingness as to a lack of understanding of the crucial nature of today's social revolution in Latin America.

Having considered these main trends of present educational development in Latin America, we would like to outline some challenges to private agencies hoping to work in Latin American education. Some of them will apply both to the private and the public sector because of the national educational needs; others will be specific challenges to the private sector.

1. First of all—and it was stated implicitly before—there cannot be a question of two educational systems, a public one and a private one. *There must be only the national educational system* because of the national educational needs. In this one system both the public and the private sector have their own responsibilities and duties. However, both sectors should work as harmoniously as possible. Otherwise, there will never be an adequate response to the educational needs of the people. Any antagonism between those responsible for public and private educational policy will be counterproductive to the common aims of all.

2. Consequently, because of the ideological problem we mentioned, *members of religious orders and congregations should move individually into the public schools.* They should do so not for proselytism but primarily for the educational needs. Even though it would not be possible to give religious instruction in the public school, as is the case in a number of pluralistic societies, this doesn't mean that it would be worthless for a religious to teach in a public school.

3. Because of the great need for community development, *private agencies should work in adult education.* To say that he who has the youth has the future is a common cliche. But is it true? Especially when we consider Latin America where general education is a long term process, too long in fact to solve immediate needs? Furthermore, long-term projects are almost impossible in Latin America for many reasons too complex to discuss here. Instead of these, all kinds of short-term programs are needed: on-the-job training programs, short complementary courses, part time courses for industrial jobs, low level management courses, instruction

in new farming techniques, secretarial classes, nurses and social workers training and, not least in importance, teacher training. There is a tremendous need for programs to teach responsible parenthood, child care, hygiene, home economics, etc. With all these examples we would not say that dealing with youth is a waste of energy, but we think that youth-education has been stressed too much to the detriment of adult education and the immediate needs for development.

4. As already has been mentioned, every educational effort should be oriented toward overall development. In the traditional school system there should be *a major effort to expand technical and agricultural training and programs in social sciences,* based on the real social doctrine of the Church. Moreover, in every school there is a need to teach an ethos of development.

5. There is also *a special task for private agencies in the experimental field.* Today we realize that the traditional school is not the only means of education. Besides adult education, there are other means which are growing in importance. The radio school systems of Latin America which started in Colombia have proven this. Until now, the use of audio-visual systems, education by correspondence and mass communication media in general have been greatly under-estimated.

6. Special attention should be given to *the integration of social classes.* This does not mean that a private school for wealthy families should have some kind of annex school for the poor as is common in many parts of Latin America today. This kind of school system emphasizes even more the social distinction between rich and poor in a number of ways very significant to sensitive children: differences in clothes, desks, teaching materials, and so on. Integration means that children of different social classes should be together in class-room as far as is possible.

The effect of such a school on the children of the upper classes will be to give a social education to them and also to their parents who do not like their children mixed with "common" people as is frequently heard among upper class Latin Americans. This kind of Christian social education is especially urgent.

7. For those who come from abroad to work in education we go back to what was said in the beginning of this paper about the differences between the two Americas. One who is a good teacher or educational expert at home is not necessarily qualified in Latin America. Too many foreigners have opened schools in Latin America that would be wonderful in their own country, but are not orientated toward national needs. Many of these schools were begun for foreigners living in Latin America but eventually most end up providing education to Latin Americans. It is common for Latin American children in these schools to learn more about the country of their teachers than about their own. When classes are given in a foreign language such as English the children develop problems in their native tongue. Hence, *foreigners must pay special attention to the needs of their new country* and spend quite a long time studying these problems before they begin actual teaching.

8. *The formation of Christians* is not a consideration to be left for last place in any education effort. Such formation *should be included in all of the previous list of challenges to the private sector:* in both public and private schools, in adult education, in programs outside formal schooling in programs using mass communications media. There should be a great effort to teach Christian social doctrine in every phase of education. An inquiry made recently discovered that in many countries students from Catholic schools were said to be well trained as students but poorly trained as Christians. So we must make a special effort to improve Christian formation even in our Catholic schools.

9. Lastly, we must lay stress on *the need for careful planning* of our effort. Time is short and teachers too scarce for us to continue improvisation which is at this moment the worst enemy of the development in Latin America. This means that everybody has to be aware of the studies that

are being done or have to be done on educational needs. It means also *coordination within the private sector itself as well as with the public sector.* The time is past, when as happened recently, a rector of a Catholic university said to one of his students that her desire to study educational planning was outside the Catholic approach because it indicated a marxist tendency. *Planning IS the key to success in Latin American education.*

CHAPTER 15

The Latin American
University Student

Rodrigo Guerrero

European and North American students are very different from Latin American students. These differences many times complicate our efforts to understand and help each other.

Our students study against a backdrop of our problems, of revolution and social change. These are things that you don't talk of in the United States. These problems are reflected in the student field in a very special way. They contribute to the differences between our students.

We need not judge these differences. But we must discuss and understand the differences.

LOW PERCENTAGES IN HIGHER STUDIES   The Latin American student is a privileged person. In any country where the level of illiteracy ranges from 30 percent to 50 percent, those people who have some education and specifically a university degree are distinctly privileged. This education makes the students a special class in our society.

In Colombia, for example, only one tenth of one percent of those who enter primary school reach the university. To achieve this university level, they must overcome many handicaps, especially economic. Many of them have to begin to work very young, some at about 12 years of age, to support their family which can mean as many as 8 or 10 people. They have to overcome the inherent problems of our schools where

196

textbooks and the techniques of education are not well developed. The student who survives these obstacles and reaches the university is a privileged person.

This is not the situation in the more highly organized societies of the United States and Europe. There education is a possibility for the majority of the people. The only obstacle to progress normally is personal limitation.

According to CEPAL (Economic Conference for Latin America) in 1957 only ten percent of the population in Argentina between 19 and 22 years, the normal age for university students, were enrolled in the Argentine universities. In the same year this percentage was two percent in the Dominican Republic and four tenths of one percent in Haiti. In Europe the figures were well over thirty percent. It is obvious then that we have a small number of people who reach the university and even fewer stay there.

This fact is sufficient to make a social leader of the Latin American student even before the conclusion of his studies.

COMPELLING FACTS MAKE RADICALS   A further and more crucial cause of student involvement is that our students, receiving a better professional training than their fellow citizens, therefore understand clearly the injustices and the problems of the society in which they live. Usually they react in a strong way against those injustices and problems.

These are the reasons why students in Latin America play a major role in politics. They have the time to be involved and they perceive the problems. They know that they are privileged and they sense a moral obligation to help solve the problems. In many cases they engage in public affairs even before leaving the university.

This is not the case with a student from a developed society where injustices and problems are not so striking or severe. In this type of culture a student can dedicate all his time to his duties at the university with the intention of reshaping society once his studies are completed.

This is a general view of the situation of most Latin American students. From a Catholic point of view there are some additional problems.

One of the most serious problems in Latin America is the massive lack of faith among students. They forsake religion during the last years of high school and remain apart from the Church during their professional and postgraduate training. In spite of our homogeneous Catholic society in Latin American countries, students almost automatically begin to lose their faith. The majority of our students abandon the ancient faith and lapse into a type of agnosticism or positivism. Religion assumes a cultural value for critical, detached study.

RELIGIOUS INSTRUCTION FAILS TO GROW UP   Religion instruction in our countries is not adapted to the intellectual level. It is presented in a childish way, based on feeling rather than reflection and thought. A student reaching intellectual maturity demands a solid basis for his beliefs. Unable to discover such, he drops his commitment. We need to develop a pastoral program for students to solve this problem before it is too late. Most of our graduate students do not practice their Catholic religion. Even those from the strongest Catholic backgrounds lose their faith when they begin to study.

Further postgraduate training for Latin American students in this country, and especially in Europe, is often not beneficial. In some cases it is certainly harmful. A number of students who come to North America and Europe have serious religious problems. Religious crises are caused by the new patterns of morality. Many Latin American girls, unaccustomed to the American ideas of freedom, without the protection of society and parents, become victims of pressures beyond their comprehension.

Many of the Latin American students are no longer Catholics when they come here. They are not practicing Catholics. Nevertheless, there is Catholicism in their hearts and if they are approached, or spoken to and have some kind of lectures or courses in what Catholicism means very many of them will come back to their faith out of this program.

EARLY ABSENCE HAS UNHEALTHY CONSEQUENCES There is a significant difference between students who finish high school in Latin American countries and come to the States to study in college and those students who graduate in Latin American universities and come to the United States for graduate studies. Those people who come for the first four years of college don't go back or if they do they don't belong to their own culture any longer because intellectually and emotionally and psychologically they have assumed the values of a different culture, that of the United States. Those people who come for their graduate studies after they finish university studies in Latin America are the ones that we should work with in the United States for they hold the greatest potential for return.

When they arrive they don't understand the culture, they don't understand the United States, they don't understand the values, they don't understand the people, they don't understand the social customs of the United States. They have to search constantly for the right course of action. They try to adjust. Those people who help them in the first stage win those Latin Americans. The organization that does something for the Latin American students, either meeting them at the port, bringing them to the campus, or inviting them to parties and social activities, wins the allegiance of the Latins. The student becomes interested in that group and recognizes that these people are taking care of him. Usually Catholic organizations at the universities don't do that.

INTELLECTUAL EFFICIENCY ABROAD IS LOW The intellectual efficiency of Latin American students in foreign countries is extremely low. The number of dropouts is astonishingly high. In many cases those who achieve good results don't want to go back to their old-fashioned and underdeveloped country. They become too identified with the country where they make the postgraduate training to return to their original country. When they are required to return by immigration laws, they fulfill the requirements and hastily leave their fatherland.

Many learn economic theories that are not well adapted for the country in which they are going to work. The economics here in the United States is quite different from the economics they will need in a developing country. Our medical students become accustomed to the high standards of medical practice here. This is a level that we cannot afford. They return to discover that they cannot work with our primitive medical system. They come back here or they live their lives dreaming of coming back.

A practical inter-American cooperation program should seek a way of assisting Latin American students to overcome these difficulties. We ought to have a plan for all aspects of student life. We must create a Catholic action program for the Latin American students. We must guide them in their technical and professional studies. We must encourage them in the love of their homeland and maintain in them a desire to return home.

MORE HOME CONTACTS WHILE ABROAD   It would be useful to have Latin American centers where they could receive newspapers, have folkloric music, and conferences and lectures on Latin American problems to keep them attached to their native country. The major universities should develop Latin American centers. We need to establish fellowships and scholarships for candidates who accept the commitment to work in their own country as soon as their studies are over.

Marxists have understood the great influence Latin American students have in their societies and have concentrated their efforts in this field. Marxists concentrate their work and invest their money in the universities and educational centers. The result is that in some Latin American countries the universities and national student unions have been the bulwark of communism and terrorism. The communists realize the political importance of Latin American student organizations and have prepared leaders to work with them.

We Catholics are now recognizing our mistake in not taking part in student life. We concentrated on studies alone. Our duty in the universities was seen as a concentration on spiritual programs. Today we are meeting the challenge and have started a vigorous student movement led by young members of the Christian Democratic Party in most of the Latin American countries. This movement is changing the situation. In Chile, for instance, the national student union is controlled by the Christian Democrats. There are other outstanding groups in Venezuela, Peru, Argentina, and Bolivia. Today there is an attempt among Catholics to participate in the whole life of the student.

GREATER TENDENCY TOWARD INTEREST IN RELIGION The students too are becoming aware of the importance of their participation as Catholics in student movements but this participation is not as efficient as necessary. Student apostolic organizations, notably the Pax Romana, JOC, and YCS movements for university students, are becoming stronger and more influential. With the help of the German hierarchy the Secretariat of Latin American Bishops (CELAM) is developing university parishes in the important student centers in Latin America. This includes training priests for this special work and, if necessary, bringing them from other countries. In some Central American countries priests are coming from Belgium and other parts of Europe. A good pastoral plan is unfolding according to the needs of the students in coordination with CELAM. It tries to encourage a Catholic action movement that impels members to become vitally engaged with the change of social structures, a change urgently needed in our countries. This is now the greatest challenge to Latin American Christians.

CHAPTER 16

Specialized Movements in the Latin American Church

Caroline Pezzullo

Latin America is in a state of economic and social revolution. So is the established Church in this revolutionary change. Catholics can be divided into three categories. The first group is ritualistic, traditional and politically conservative. A large number of Catholics in Latin America fall into this category.

The second category unites a new generation of social minded Christians who are setting up social services and institutions under the inspiration of Christian social thought.

The third embraces the committed Christian or the Christian who sees the need for training people for action in a pluralistic society rather than for a transformation of society through creation of Christian structures. This Christian looks for the means of preparing leaders at all levels to spearhead Latin America's social and economic revolution. Marina Bandeira, for example, can be located in this third category. But people like Marina represent such a minority that they are in effect, almost a prophetic element. They may be among those who in part inspired Pope John's encyclical, *Peace on Earth*.

FIVE PER CENT IN ACTIVE APOSTOLATE   Of the twenty per cent good Catholics in Latin America (debatable percentage by the way) probably five per cent are actively engaged in the apostolate of the Church. The formation of this apostolate in Latin America is patterned very much after the Mexican general Catholic Action Movement, that is, an organization on parochial, diocesan and national levels involving Catholic men and women and Catholic youth. This pattern was adopted in all of the countries of Latin America with the exception of Brazil which started out concentrating on specialized movements.

Let us now consider the field of specialized Catholic action This movement originated from the Young Christian Workers, an international youth organization formed of working people. The founder is the newly appointed Cardinal Cardijn. (In the United States I understand the name has recently been changed to Young Christian Movement.)

The Young Christian Workers are concerned chiefly with the preparation of Christian leaders who will work in a pluralist society toward the full development of social institutions. They are not necessarily challenging the faulty structures of society with a view toward complete revolution and complete change. Rather, they are looking for what is called in Latin America "revindication."

However, specialized movements have filled a providential need in Latin America.

Within the last decade they have gained momentum with the Young Christian Workers, the Adult Christian Worker Movement, the Young Christian Student Movements (organized on high school and university levels), the Agricultural Workers, the Christian Family Movement, which has grown very rapidly throughout the continent, and UNIA-PAC, a specialized movement of employers and businessmen just getting under way in various parts of the continent.

EUROPE INFLUENCES SPECIALIZED MOVEMENTS The approach of these specialized movements is basically patterned after those of Europe from where they originated. Small groups of similar backgrounds and interests, organized on parochial, diocesan and national levels.

In Latin America the great mass of people are unemployed

or under employed. The middle and upper classes constitute a small minority. For this reason, it was rather difficult in the general Catholic Action movement, operating as it did among the middle and upper classes, to recruit working people and do it in a non-paternalistic fashion. Therefore, the specialized movements answered the need for centralizing on the person and his environment. What the specialized movements offered, I think, was actually what Monsignor (now Cardinal) Cardijn offered to the whole Church: a new era of social minded Christians; the idea that the poorest workers have not only a role in history but a dynamic role in the Church and in their environment. In short that they not only labor for the Church, but that they *are* the Church.

Specialized movements also place emphasis on the layman and his role in the social order, and not just within the establishment of the Church. Perhaps the most important aspect of this has been the crystallizing of the inquiry method: see-judge-and-act as a form of action and as a training for action. We may say parenthetically that Pope John pointed to this method as today's great instrument for Christian Action.

Through this plan of action the layman relates and becomes fully acquainted with his own reality. He looks upon this reality in the light of the teachings of Christ and the scripture.

A few summary remarks on the specialized movements at the technical and professional levels. The need exists for a movement which will give Christian training and impetus to the social revolution on all levels in the Church. But obviously such a movement cannot be brought about through social action alone; the cooperative for example, whatever else may characterize it, should be a pluralistic enterprise.

SPECIALIZED MOVEMENTS DEFICIENT IN INFLUENCE At the moment specialized movements are not really answering the need of relating the message of the Gospel to the new groups of technocrats, planners and other professionals. One reason is because the movements do not always attract leaders who are in the mainstream of social change. Often those heading the movements don't see the necessity of making a connection between the militant action of its leaders and the needs and revolutionary process of society as a whole. This is a big drawback rarely challenged. It is certainly not being faced realistically in this country or in a number of other countries that I've had the privilege of observing.

Another reason is that some specialized movements are limited to the middle class. This criticism has been applied to the Christian Family Movement. CFM leadership, on the other hand, claims that the couples come from classes in which the problems of the family life are not directly related to the need for radical social changes. I think that this is a very important consideration when you recall that we've been trying to examine the social revolution in Latin America and we are asking if the structures that the Church has already established are really going to be able to do a proper job.

In Brazil, a country I know best in Latin America, many student leaders are moving into pluralist organizations. They are doing this as a result of the impetus given them by the specialized movements. Because of the richness of their formation in the specialized movements they have been able to contribute to causes championed by people with no professed religious affiliation: a good thing, provided the concepts one finds in the specialized movement are not rejected; and hence, no formation provided for future generations.

BETTER RELATION TO CURRENT NEEDS Generally speaking, specialized movements have to take a long hard look at themselves if they wish to relate to the needs of our age. They are not working all that smoothly. I feel that our specialized movements will have to reach other levels of people than they are now influencing; professionals, technicians, local and national planners. But for the time being they are the best available.

In conclusion, we of North America have a tremendous amount to learn from Latin America. The nationalist movement for independence in Africa has given a tremendous impetus to the civil rights movement in this country. There is a definite connection between the African experience and the tactics in Latin America.

Similarly, I feel that our fraternal involvement with Latin America and with those Latin American organizations specifically within the Church, can have a revolutionary effect on the membership of the Church in North America.

The acceleration of Latin America's development triggered by its people's search for a better way of life has in some ways made Latin America closely attuned to what is coming out of the Ecumenical Council, particularly in its directives for the layman. We can learn much from them on how to create new life in the American Church, how to involve and train Catholics on a parish or extra-parochial level for the great tasks of our rapidly changing society. For unless we do something in this direction now—those whom we eventually send to work in Latin America will not be able to relate to the committed Catholic in that area. This is not to judge the quality of people who go abroad—not at all. Their commitment is obvious if they're willing to give up the comforts of their homes. But for our committed Catholic to relate successfully to Latin America's committed Catholic it would help greatly if we could learn from the Latin American Church the secret of the tremendous Christian renewal which so many of its sons and daughters have experienced in the revolutionary context of their own lives.

CHAPTER 17

Latin America's Christian Family Movement

Pedro Richards, C.P.

I would like to begin by an acknowledgement of the help which the Christian Family Movement in Latin America received from the Christian Family Movement in the USA. In 1952 when we made our start, I received inspiration from the United States which supplemented what I picked up in France. You will see that among our literature, one of the booklets is a Spanish translation of what CFM people in the U.S. call the yellow book. Hence I give you only your due when I express our gratitude.

It is in *Pacem in Terris* that John XXIII, who used to like to recall the happy family life he led (there were 30 family members under his roof), stated that the family is the natural and essential basis of society. As Bishop Prata of La Paz said in the Council, we must change our idea that the parish should be considered the ecclesiastical bottom organization. The parish is the basic ecclesiastical organization but the supernaturalized cell of the Church which is the family is the bedrock of the Mystical Body.

IDEOLOGIES INFLUENCE FAMILY LIFE The family in Latin America has been sorely tried. The key to understanding Latin America as regards the family is the impact which ideologies have made upon it. If this is not understood, it will be difficult for those who come among us to apply the proper remedies that fit our particular family. Remember, it is not a family of Africa or a family of Asia. Ours is a family which was Christian and was assailed by ideologies in the last century which have deprived it of its supernatural heritage. Individualistic ideologies have introduced inside our family dissociation and atomizing elements, destroying the family which should be a community. Collective ideologies, then, have often made our family a pauper of society, a real Cinderella. Our constitutions based on the French Revolution and hence individualistic in philosophy do not consider the family as do modern constitutions in Europe. For example, we have already eleven ministries of family affairs in governments of Europe. There's one in Canada too, which means to say that alongside of ministries of finance and ministries for food and social affairs at last the family is finding its particular niche too.

The family is likewise suffering from the current of social change which is sweeping over Latin America. It has been said that the family is a sounding board; undoubtedly if we have ears to hear and sufficient sensibility, we experience within a family what is going on in the street, what's going on in Parliament, what's being written in the newspapers, what is seen on TV or at the cinema. Hence the technological reform which is happening in Latin America is affecting the family. For instance, when the petroleum fields were given out to international companies under Frondizi's government in Argentina, no provision was made for the families of the workers. Hence workers were attracted by high wages from different parts of the country but they were forced to leave their families behind. Similarly in the case of the braceros who came over the border from Mexico into California as cheap labor to pick fruit, cotton and vegetables. Their family life was weakened because the technical structure which enticed the bracero did not take his family into consideration.

INDUSTRIAL REVOLUTION HITS FAMILY LIFE   Family life likewise is affected through the industrial revolution sweeping over our continent. People leave the land in order to settle in major cities such as Buenos Aires, Sao Paulo and Mexico City and the structure of the family itself is influenced profoundly.

Urban society is bringing down birth rates, making the family less stable, making those who were peasants yesterday the victims of many ideological currents of thought found in the city and not on the land.

In order to understand what is happening to the family we must make a diagnosis. We must know what therapeutics are to be applied; unless we know the ailment it will be difficult to apply the remedy. Those who go down to Latin America must realize that unless the condition of the family is straightened out it is useless to propose economic structures or to erect parishes or to seek vocations for the religious or priestly life.

FOUR KEY SOLUTIONS   What are the solutions? I would point out four aspects here—First of all, there is the need of education for love. I'm not saying education for marriage; I speak of the need to educate for love, I refer to that difficult age that begins at times in our tropical countries not at 12 but at 11 or 10, an attraction toward the other sex. We need parents who will create a climate of integrity inside their homes and deliberately form their children. The school must cooperate as well as the parish and youth movements, so that they'll make a proper use of love. One of the remedies for our high birth rate is to put back to a normal age the formation of homes and not have such early marriages as very often we have on our continent. This is part of formation. This is part of a campaign to make them realize that they cannot play at love; they cannot choose a partner for life at such an early age as 15, 16 or 17.

The members of our Movimiento Familiar Cristiano go to the high schools and give two short courses in the first years of high school. We call this a vocational course. Vocation mustn't be identified only with vocations to the religious or the priestly life because every human being has a vocation just as every human being has sex. There is a vocation to married life as there is a vocation to virginity consecrated to Christ in the world. This course is given so that boys and girls will realize that each is called to love in one or other of a three-fold manner: either collaborating with God the Father in matrimony, or collaborating with God the Son in the priesthood, or collaborating with God the Holy Ghost by consecrating their virginity either in an official manner in religious life or as so many people, volunteers and others, like the Papal Volunteers do by going to Latin America. They consecrate themselves privately to extend God's kingdom through social action, through a career or otherwise.

A second course is given in high school which prepares our youth for family life. Our men go to the schools for boys and women go to girls' high schools and in eight talks delivered successively treat of the problem of a choice of a partner. Sacramental, sexual, physiological, economic and legal aspects of marriage are covered as well as liturgical and cultural behavior.

THE ROLE OF PRE-CANA A third aspect should be taken into consideration in preparation for marriage and here, once again, the members of the Movimiento Familiar Cristiano play a role. This time it is through Pre-Cana, because in Latin America we embrace in the Movimiento not only married couples but the Cana conferences. The conferences and retreats are for engaged and married couples as well as for groups of widows to develop that spirituality which was so wonderfully explained by Pius XII in his famous discourse of September 1957.

This preparation for marriage must, as you well know, embrace sexual adaptation. We must give youth this training in periodical continence for three reasons. First of all, so that they realize that sex is not something impulsive but rather something which in a rational being must be controlled by his reason or by his faith. Secondly, because they must have personal experience that they cannot only observe continence but likewise realize how each particular couple works with regard to rhythm. And thirdly, to oblige them to realize that there are other dimensions to their conjugal relations apart from the sexual relations. There are psychological relations and supernatural ones as well.

ATTENTION TO TENSIONS Further, in this preparation for marriage the need must be cited for conjugal harmony; something in this field has to be attained in consummate fashion. As a basic safeguard to living, each day must begin with its prayer for harmony because tensions in family life are ever present quite as there is tension between our body and soul and between this world and the world to come.

Each couple likewise requires conditioning in the need to keep up the home that has been formed because it is one thing to get married and another thing to keep married. Three-fourths of divorces happen, according to world statistics, before the fifteenth year of marriage. Half of these divorces occur before the tenth year of marriage while the heaviest portion of divorces take place between the fifth and tenth year of marriage. Hence married couples need to join what can be called therapeutical groups because if they're ill, they'll be cured and if they're not ill, the groups will serve as a sort of vaccine to keep them from getting the disease which assails other families and other groups who fail to keep up their family youth.

A VERITABLE CELL IN CHURCH LIFE We labor ceaselessly that the Latin American family will become a veritable cell of the Church, first of all in a sacramental union. Unfortunately a high percentage of families in certain countries are not formed sacramentally. We need, then, to sacramentalize families and keep them sacramental. We must always remember that marriage is a sacrament of the living and must be lived in grace if it is to become operative. But this involves a problem when we think that religiously only 10% of Latin Americans go to Sunday Mass. Naturally this embraces those who are living up in the cordillera or in forests far away from the possibility of attending Mass.

Happily, a movement of spiritual exercises for engaged and married couples has spread out through Latin America —weekend retreats, cursillos for married couples, not man and wife separately but man and wife together, both gathered in the same spirituality. In Mexico we have gone so far as to have married couples make eight day retreats together. This is the awakening of the Church in Latin America. If we will only go further than looking at the economic structures, we will realize there is a level being formed in Latin America which will raise that continent to unsuspected heights.

Of immense importance is the role of the man in the Latin American family. The husband must be the Christ of his home; he must be its leader, its prophet, its priest. Religion is transmitted by the family. When a family becomes femininely accentuated, that is to say, when the woman alone practices religion and not the man, religion then becomes feminine as well and this unfortunately has led to the success of secularism in Latin American lands. In Mexico, for instance, with no man to fight the family's religious battles, Church property was confiscated in the last century; as of 1936 Cardenas confiscated Catholic schools and open persecution continued for years.

SOCIAL STRUCTURES DON'T JUST HAPPEN   Now we come finally to the family movements. Social structures don't merely happen and the Christian Family Movement hasn't forgotten the community life outside the home. This family is responsible for the coming, the training, the upholding, the orientation of the human person. There is no structure as important as the family. What's the use of having paved streets or TV or having family wages if we haven't got the family? Hence the need of not forgetting the family. And as Pius XII said, the community is for the family. But today under the impact of philosophical liberalism we have a community which is not family centered. Yet this is the aim which family movements have around the world. You in the United States and we in Latin America aim to get a community family-minded, not merely person-minded.

And so the family has this triple relationship, the relation of a man and wife (conjugal relationship), the relation of parents and child (educational relationship), and the relation of the family as a whole to relatives, neighbors, community—Catholics, Protestants, agnostics, atheists. The law of love is a law of neighborliness.

Today, to bring down the matter to statistics, the Christian Family Movement is the involvement of 30,000 married couples throughout Latin America. We have approximately 8,000 in Argentina, 5,000 in Brazil, 1,500 in Chile, 50 in Nicaragua, 1,700 in Uruguay, 1,500 in Venezuela. Mexico has been really such an extraordinary success that in the recent national assembly a few days ago there were 1,600 representatives from 52 of the 57 dioceses and in three days we had 8,000 communions. Since they were communions of married couples, there were 4,000 men. No other movement in Latin America has mobilized men so successfully as has the Christian Family Movement. Why? Because they have been given exactly what they wanted. They have been told how to love and how to be saved through love.

CHAPTER 18

Latin America
and the Universal Church

Most Rev. Manuel Larraín

It is my desire that through friendly exchange Americans and Latin Americans come to understand one another better. With this in mind I am going to condense our subject into three ideas: a question, an analysis and an appeal.

THE CATHOLIC CONSCIENCE OF THE WORLD   Latin America above all presents a question which confronts the Catholic conscience of the world and can be thus formulated: what is the meaning of this fraction of the world to the universal Church?

This question is a concrete expression of the Catholic conscience and our solidarity in Christ. To ignore it would betray a lack of vision of the Church and the world.

Not to find an answer to it would imply that the mystery of redemption was not understood in all its vastness.

Let us then try to uncover this answer:

a. *Numerically* speaking, Latin America embraces almost a third of the Catholic Church, a proportion which will be even greater at the end of this century.

b. *Historically* speaking, Latin America is a continent born to civilization under the religious symbol of Catholicism; a continent whose development has been accompanied by the Church at each step of its history; a continent whose oldest tradition reflects a strong Christian inspiration that constitutes its richest potential of energy.

214

c. *Sociologically,* Latin America represents and, one might say, synthesizes the great challenge between material development and Christianity. It places before humanity the great question: is Catholicism capable of directing Latin America towards the human development it so urgently requires? Will this development justify or weaken the Christian position? This is a formidable challenge to which an answer must be given without further delay by the present generation.

d. From a *missionary* point of view, Latin America represents for the universal Church a most significant and urgent field of action. It confronts all Catholics with this question: what is more important, to bring new men to the life of Christ, or to help to preserve the faith of those who already possess it?

LATIN AMERICA IS LATIN AMERICA   The original question keeps repeating itself: what is the meaning of this fraction of the world for the universal Church? The answers we have given from the standpoint of numbers, history, sociology and missions reveal a new aspect: the perennial message of the Gospel is assuming new cultural forms, in human groups that are acquiring a new physiognomy. This fact should be emphasized once again: Latin America is neither a European, North American nor African civilization. Latin America is Latin America and the human expression of its Christianity, its temporal existence, should necessarily reflect that reality.

In this respect, two different problems arise. For Latin American Catholics, an effort must be made to incorporate the thought, the practices of the universal Church in autochthonous forms according to the character, history and human reality of our people. North American and European countries which are collaborating with us with such great love and fraternal charity must seek a psychological and pastoral adaptation which is inherent to any authentically missionary action. It is not enough that Vatican II has given us the use of a vernacular language for our liturgy; Latin America is also in great need of a vernacular pastoral program.

We repeat the same question: what is the meaning of Latin America for the universal Church?

The answer forces us to face our tremendously serious ecumenical responsibility.

An unescapable dilemma arises from Latin America. It could reveal a tragic failure of a Christian inspired civilization, which would tell the countries of the "third world" that the Church is unable to give them and their people the human and spiritual development they require. Conversely Latin America could become the fulfillment of one of the dearest hopes of the Church of tomorrow: a new continent, with new energies, open to all the innovations that the hour demands.

THE LETTER MUST NOT KILL THE SPIRIT   Latin America with its impetuous growth is reminding us that the modern world is developing at a faster rate than our institutions, which in turn creates the danger that the institutions might suffocate worthy development. The letter must not kill the spirit; the fundamental structures should lead but not constrain a Church which should go and meet the world to give it what is expected from her: the redeeming action of Christ.

Hence the dilemma of Latin America is enlarged and becomes a problem for the Catholic conscience, a test of authentic missionary spirit and a proof of the true understanding of the meaning and spirit of Vatican II.

In reality, it all amounts to verifying whether we fully understand the fact that the Church is the communion in Christ of all mankind; whether Catholics of 1965 are willing to accompany the march of the Church which Vatican II has just shown us as its great and universal purpose.

At the beginning I mentioned that the subject of Latin America's role in the world Church brings up a question. I also added that it required an analysis. This analysis should be undertaken in the light of two realities: that of Latin America itself, and that related to the position of the universal Church.

ANALYSIS OF THE REALITY OF LATIN AMERICA This demands a thorough knowledge of the real physiognomy of Latin America. Let us be honest about it: in general Latin America is either completely unknown or very slightly known.

An analysis shows that the first century of the evangelization of the Latin American continent represented the greatest missionary and civilizing enterprise in the history of the Church. A consideration of this evangelization helps us to learn much about the qualities, deficiencies and possibilities of Latin American Catholicism.

Its *qualities* include the deep faith which has overcome the enormous difficulties the Church in Latin America has had to face in the last 150 years; the spirit of charity expressed in a simple and generous hospitality; the sense of providence which in the midst of hardship and anguish never permits mistrust of the Father in heaven; and the austerity of a hard life which embraces the mystery of the Cross.

Its *deficiencies* are a frequent absence of properly adequate evangelization; an excessive devotion to the sentimental rather than to the doctrinal; a lack of an adequate structuring of its pastoral program; a scarcity of clergy.

Its *possibilities* reveal a desire for pastoral renewal; for an embodiment of the social doctrine of the Church; an immense effort for revival of vigorous Catholic life that her episcopate, clergy and faithful are making at the present moment. Its leaders tell us that in the Church of Latin America there exists a phenomenal youthful spiritual and apostolic renewal which could well be extended to other countries with an older Christian tradition.

This analysis will make us realize that what the Church of Latin America really needs is greater trust in her ability to rebuild herself and greater understanding that the present moment is desperate and grave, yet full of promising expectations.

An analysis should guide us in the interpretation of facts and of people in the light of their history, their idiosyncracies and their ethnic and social characteristics, in order not to impose apostolic forms and styles which are foreign to our ways and to our thinking.

The analysis should let us see the special significance of every effort for personnel or material aid that we give to this continent, which we can well call a "land of anguish and hope."

THE MISSION OF THE UNIVERSAL CHURCH   This analysis should be carried out in the light of the problems of the universal Church.

The Council has demonstrated to us the immense missionary prospects opened before our horizon.

The people of God advance through history. The role of the whole Church—hierarchy, priesthood and laymen—is to carry out that great missionary work of our century which Cardinal Suhard stated in prophetic words: in a world that is unifying itself in its material aspect, the unification of the spiritual is imperative. Who will effect this spiritual unity of the world? We listen to the eternal reply of Christ: "I am the light of the world." "I have come to give life."

It is in the light of this great missionary aim that we should examine the problem of Latin America in the universal Church.

Latin America cannot and will not continue to be a Church which only receives. She knows she has work to do for the missionary Church that spreads everywhere the message of Christ. Through her anguish and her deprivations she is to-day already contributing to the universal Church in her bitter sufferings.

In the Church of the poor to which John XXIII referred in his inaugural speech before the Council and which Paul VI mentioned in his first encyclical, the Church of Latin

America stands as a sign and declaration that the mere material value of what is given is not what renders an action profitable. She knows that when colonialism disappears in other continents, the priests who will be most welcome will not be those who come from the former colonial nations but those who, like Latin America's priests, are "citizens of the third world," the world of underdevelopment.

She knows that if today she is passing through a difficult moment she may become, thanks to the understanding of her brothers and sisters of many nations, a strong force at the service of the whole Church, as was declared by Popes Pius XII and John XXIII.

PURPOSES OF THIS ANALYSIS   This analysis should be directed to the study of attitudes towards the Church of Latin America. I myself am a Latin American and feel proud to say so. I know Latin America, her history, her bizarre geography, her anguish, her miseries and her strivings. But above all, I know the Latin American person and I assure the world that there is nothing we appreciate so much as the fact that people trust us. Hence the need of regarding our problems with the certainty that we are capable of solving them, provided that in a given moment we receive the cooperation we need.

The analysis must create a confidence in us, a confidence that must lead to dialogue. The dialogue requires an understanding that Latin America has a word to say in the historic hour the Church is now facing and that that word must be heard because it is God who speaks in history. That word may perhaps lack something in experience and human strength, but it has nevertheless the freshness of sincerity and the seal of authentic earnestness. It comes from a continent whose problems make it more apt to undertake the renewal which this hour so critical for the world and the Church demands from all Catholics.

AN APPEAL TO MEN OF GOOD WILL   A question, an analysis,

and an appeal. We have dealt with the first two items. I must now refer to the third one. And before the appeal we must ask a new question: who is calling?

It is now ten years since Pius XII convoked Latin America's bishops at the historic meeting of Rio de Janeiro, from which emerged not only a vision of the general problems of Latin America's Church but above all, the decision to face them with the calm confidence of those who are not overcome by obstacles but put their trust in God. Like the shepherd of the Moab mountains, the Latin American Church convoked by her supreme Chief answered to the great problems presented: "I come in the name of the Lord of hosts." Therefrom the Latin American Episcopal Council (CELAM) was born.

As John XXIII started his pontificate we can report that the first act of his government was to speak to Latin America, addressing a portion of its episcopate gathered in Rome for the third session of CELAM.

In his last hours on earth, then, while his lips uttered his final prayers, his recollections and blessings flew toward our continent. With filial pride, we may say that we were the first and the last in his thoughts—the first fruits of his life as Pope and the final recipients of his blessing as Universal Shepherd.

Now his successor, Paul VI, constantly displays his concern, affection and interest for this continent—"Christian but menaced," as he expresses it.

We can therefore reply without hesitation to the question; who is calling? It is the Pope, the successor of Peter, the one who has "the solicitude of all the churches."

Who is calling? It is Latin America itself that is calling. It is the same as in St. Paul's vision, when he saw a Macedonian appealing to him—"Come over and help us." The Church of Latin America repeats the identical sentence to all her brothers in Christendom.

THE PLEA OF THE LATIN AMERICAN CHURCH   Although it may

seem paradoxical, we ask for help because we are conscious of our strength as well as our weakness, because we feel sure that God would not have deposited such enormous reserves of faith, hope and love in a continent where there is this reserve, if it were not for placing them at the disposal of all men and all the Church.

We ask for help, not because we wish to receive, but on the contrary, because we want to give. Because we wish more and more to become a living power in Christ's Mystical Body. Because in the hour of the Council we were conscious of being a part of the pilgrim Church that makes progress amidst the anxieties and problems of a developing world.

Who is calling? It is the Church of Vatican II dialoguing with the world; seeking in the light of doctrine a vision of man that may be the answer to the great uncertainties of all mankind. The Church does not want weak spots within her body but wishes that all may concur in the fulfillment of her universal mission.

And this is an appeal which is not only concerned with spiritual problems, but also with the most anguishing social problem of our America: underdevelopment.

It is true that the fundamental mission of the Church is spiritual and religious but it is also true that in the fulfillment of that mission the essential problems of man are involved: liberty, justice, solidarity and peace. A spiritual advance which is not intimately connected with human development cannot be postulated.

Spiritual progress would not be consistent unless it were accompanied by social progress. The equation of temporal action and spiritual action, of the energies of the world and the Church, seem to gather in Latin America to give us a vision of a Church which must be intimately present to God in its evangelizing task, and, as well, authentically present to men in its civilizing action. Here the two spheres—the human and the religious—are brought together by a deeper unity which should constantly be rediscovered and realigned.

LATIN AMERICA AND THE UNIVERSAL CHURCH A question, an analysis, and an appeal. This is what we have sought to present.

Our goal is epitomized in the words of John XXIII to Cardinal Lienart: "The future of those vast regions depends upon the effort carried out in their favor by the ensemble of the Church."

It is a universal task, as far-reaching as the mission of the Church. The answer to the question, to the analysis, and to the call, will make it possible for the men of the America of the southern half of our Western Hemisphere, freed from injustice, to raise their eyes to the heavens and envision the Southern Cross shining there as a sign of hope.

DISCUSSION OUTLINE

prepared by

Vaile Scott
Executive Director
Catholic Adult Education Center
Archdiocese of Chicago

SECTION I—SOCIO-CULTURAL CONSIDERATIONS

Latin America and the United States—A Social Confrontation, Abbé François Houtart (Page 3)

1. Explain and discuss the difference in methods of colonization in North America and Latin America which Father Houtart describes. What were the motives that caused these differences?
2. Describe the basis of power for each of the four groups who shared economic, social, political and cultural power after the conquest of Latin America. Discuss how this power structure affected the social situation in Latin America.
3. Does a comparison of the development of the social structure in northern and southern colonies of North America indicate that this structure was any more humane than the structure which was developed in Latin America? Consider its effect on the native Indians and Negroes.
4. What are the major factors which account for the failure of the political revolutions in Latin America to achieve independence?
5. Explain what Father Houtart means when he says the Church in Latin America is in a very difficult situation.
6. Discuss the significance of the main lines of the confrontation between the two parts of the Western hemisphere which Father Houtart summarizes.

The Social Crisis in Latin America, Rev. Roger Vekemans, S. J. (Page 26)

1. Why does Father Vekemans ask the question, "Latin America, does it exist or not?"
2. Do you agree with Father Vekemans' analysis of Latin America as a middle class continent? Explain.
3. Why does the population shift from rural to urban areas in Latin America create such a severe problem?
4. Father Vekemans says that one of his fears has to do with

population growth. How does he think this problem can be overcome?

5. In view of the author's view, why is marxism not as great a danger as it was ten years ago? What does he see as the danger now?

SECTION II—POLITICAL CONSIDERATIONS

The Phenomenon of Dictatorship, Rev. Renato Poblete, S.J. (Page 38)

1. Explain in concrete terms the meaning of political hypertrophy.
2. Describe the type of society favorable to the caudillo.
3. Why does Father Poblete state that Chile was unique in its advancement toward national consciousness and unity?
4. Discuss the role of such pressure groups as the army, the Church, and student groups on the formation of dictatorships.
5. How can foreign powers best relate to social and political upheavals within a country where a dictatorship is likely to emerge?
6. Is it valid to compare the history of dictatorships in Latin America to the current political situation in the emerging nations of Africa and Asia?

Christian Democracy and Social Reality, Rafael Caldera (Page 54)

1. Dr. Caldera (as well as several other contributors to this volume) cites the economic disadvantage which results when a nation depends solely on the production of raw materials for its economy. Can you explain this problem? What responsibility do the economically developed countries have toward those nations on whom they depend for raw materials?
2. Compare Dr. Caldera's analysis of per capita income with that of Father Vekemans in a previous chapter.
3. In what respects are the Democratic Socialists and the

Christian Democrats similar in their aims and objectives? How do they differ?

4. How do Latin American political parties differ from the type of political parties we know in the United States?

5. What does Dr. Caldera mean when he says that the Christian Democratic party does not have a confessional character?

6. What are some of the misgivings North Americans and Europeans have had toward the Christian Democratic party in Latin America?

Communists and Other Marxists, Rev. Héctor Samperio G. (Page 75)

1. Father Samperio says that communists draw their best leaders from which classes in Latin American society? What explanation does he give for this?

2. What are the four most important strategies used by the communists in Latin America?

3. Discuss the potential of communism in Latin America as it is presented by Father Samperio.

4. Explain the conditions that are unfavorable to marxism.

SECTION III—SOCIO-ECONOMIC CONSIDERATIONS

Christian Social Movement in Latin America, Marina Bandeira (Page 89)

1. Does your own interpretation and explanation of the history of social movements and human progress lead you to agree with Miss Bandeira's analysis? Can you think of important modern writers who disagree with this analysis?

2. Is the author implying that the Christian social movement is the only valid institution in Latin America working for social improvement? Explain.

3. Compare the author's remarks on community living and planning and cosmopolitan and planetarian man with her statement that "we are living in a rapidly disintegrating society . . . this is a fact."

4. Does the author give a satisfactory explanation of the role of social Protestantism in relation to the Christian Social movement?
5. Discuss Miss Bandeira's over-all analysis of ideological groups.
6. Who does Miss Bandeira want to be the arbiter in determining which are the authentic Latin American organizations capable of pulling Latin America from its underdeveloped state?

Capitalism in Latin America, James A. Hart (Page 102)

1. Discuss Dr. Hart's opening remarks in which he contrasts capitalism and communism as completely opposite systems. Is this point of view enlightening?
2. How would you evaluate the Venezuela story? Is there reason for optimism in Dr. Hart's account of capitalism in Venezuela?
3. Discuss the role of the Christian Democratic party in the political development of Venezuela.

Agrarian Reform in Latin America, Hugo Jordan (Page 111)

1. Is land ownership the only way or necessarily the best way of incorporating the laborers into the economy and providing them with political power?
2. Discuss Mr. Jordan's observation that large property does not favor development of technology. How does this compare with what is happening in North American agricultural industry? How does he evaluate the success of land distribution in Latin America?
3. What does the author mean by national integration?
4. Why does Mr. Jordan not discuss the shift of population from the rural areas to the city?
5. Mr. Jordan says, and other contributors to this volume support his view, that the solution to the Latin American problem cannot be imported but must be searched for by

Latin Americans in accord with the Latin American reality. Is this an important consideration?

6. Discuss Mr. Jordan's evaluation of the Alliance for Progress.

Christians and Workers' Movements, William C. Doherty, Jr. (Page 123)

1. Describe the fundamental ideological differences between ORIT and CLASC, expressed in this section.
2. Discuss the defense of CLASC presented in the remarks of N. Leynse excerpted from LABOR (issue number 2, 1965). Does Mr. Doherty meet these objections in his presentation?
3. Why are CLASC unions anti-United States? What does Mr. Leynse mean when he says, "A mere bread and butter trade union has no future in Latin America"?
4. Discuss the comments made by Mr. Ramón Venegas at the end of this section regarding the great misunderstanding between us.

Christian Participation in National Planning, René Otero (Page 139)

1. Do you agree with the opening remarks made by Mr. Otero that economic planning by the state is essential to growth and development?
2. How does Mr. Otero answer his own question, "Is there a place for the concept of Christian participation in social planning?" Do you agree with his answer?
3. Explain the distinction Mr. Otero makes between pastoral planning under church control and planning social development.

SECTION IV—RELIGIO-SOCIAL CONSIDERATIONS

The Church and Social Revolution in Latin America, Most Rev. Mark G. McGrath, C.S.C. (Page 149)

1. What does Bishop McGrath mean by a theology of progressive change?

2. Do you think that Vatican Council II has been an influence on the concept of progressive change?
3. Discuss the terms, "Christian revolution," "social revolution," and "pacific revolution" as they are defined by the author.
4. How does progressive change affect the concept of social revolution?
5. Should the Church as an institution directly promote programs of economic and social betterment?
6. Does this mean that the Church takes part in revolutions?

The Bright Light of Progress, Juan Cardinal Landázuri Ricketts (Page 169)

1. Of those signs of progress reported by Cardinal Landázuri, which do you consider the most hopeful?
2. Do you agree with Cardinal Landázuri's assessment of the major problems the Church currently faces?
3. Discuss the kind of help he thinks Latin America still requires.
4. Despite the improved image of the Church in Latin America, what are the two major problems Cardinal Landázuri cites? Do you think the Church in North America is making a significant contribution to the resolution of these problems?

Latin America's Bishops—Our Bond to Their Burdens, Joseph Cardinal Ritter (Page 179)

1. Why does Cardinal Ritter think the tide is turning in favor of the preservation and future flowering of Latin American Catholicism?
2. Discuss the basic attitude needed by those who wish to help assist the Church in Latin America.
3. Describe Cardinal Ritter's proposals for cooperating with Latin America and discuss his pledge to send 10 percent of the clergy of the St. Louis Archdiocese to Latin America by 1975.

Private Education in Latin America, Rev. Isaac Th. J. Wust and Rev. Gustavo Pérez (Page 187)

1. Evaluate Father Wust's statement that "we need more than a development of education; we need education for development." Do the specific examples he gives help to understand the statement?
2. Discuss each of the nine challenges to the private sector of education. Which of these do you think are most important?

The Latin American University Student, Rodrigo Guerrero (Page 196)

1. Discuss the reasons why Latin American students play a larger role in politics than North American students.
2. Consider the problem which arises when Latin American students studying in North America decide to remain here. How can this problem be solved?
3. Why do marxists pay so much attention to student groups?

Specialized Movements in the Latin American Church, Caroline Pezzullo (Page 202)

1. Describe the theory upon which the specialized movements are based.
2. Compare the specialized movement approach with that of the Christian Democratic movement in Latin America.
3. Do you think the approach of the specialized movements can be reconciled with the Christian Democratic movement described in other sections of this volume?
4. How do you interpret Miss Pezzullo's comment that the specialized movements are not really answering the need of relating the message of the Gospel to the technologists, planners, and other professionals?

Latin America's Christian Family Movement, Rev. Pedro Richards, C. P. (Page 207)

1. Consider the social structures which affect family life in

Latin America, as they are described by Father Richards. How do they compare with the social structures in the United States?

2. What effect do these differences have on family life on both continents?

3. Discuss Father Richards' theology of marriage as it relates to the world of man and woman.

4. Is the CFM an effective method in countries where family life is weak or little value is placed on the stability of marriage?

Latin America and the Universal Church, Most Rev. Manuel Larraín (Page 214)

1. How would you answer Bishop Larraín's great question, "Is Catholicism capable of directing Latin America toward the human development it so urgently requires?"

2. What is the third world Bishop Larraín refers to?

3. Bishop Larraín strikes a prophetic note in his analysis of the reality of Latin America. What meaning would you ascribe to his remarks?

4. Discuss the paradox in Bishop Larraín's plea, "We ask for help, not because we wish to receive but on the contrary because we want to give."

APPENDIX

APOSTOLIC LETTER
of
HIS HOLINESS POPE PAUL VI
to
RICHARD CARDINAL CUSHING,
Chairman Bishops' Committee for Latin America
January 6, 1965

Our venerable predecessor, John XXIII, in his autograph letter addressed to you, Beloved Son, on April 19, 1963, after expressing warm appreciation for the achievements in apostolic collaboration with the countries of Latin America, gave assurance of His firm confidence "that the American dioceses and Religious congregations will, in the years ahead, fulfill with solicitude the various more extended programs which have been proposed."

Two years later, We are happy to note that this confidence has been amply justified and those lively hopes fulfilled. Our own certitude on the subject was justly confirmed by the Second Biennial Report on the Cooperation of the Church in the United States in supplying personnel to the Church in Latin America. This document came to Us as a previous gift at Christmas time, and was a further proof, if any were

---

Archbishop Antonio Samore of Vatican City, Vice President of the Pontifical Commission for Latin America, presented a holograph letter addressed by Pope Paul VI to Cardinal Cushing at the Wednesday night session (January 27, 1965) of the CICOP Conference in Chicago. Father Louis Colonnese, Administrative Director of the Latin America Bureau of the Bishops' Committee for Latin America, read the letter to the assembly.

needed, of the devotion and attachment of the hierarchy, clergy and Catholics of the United States of America to this Apostolic See.

We read this report with lively attention, finding therein abundant statistics manifesting the generous contribution of American Catholics to the apostolate in Latin America, useful conclusions regarding the work accomplished, and courageous forecasts of the future. Above and beyond the expressive and significant figures, We were gratified to note the spirit and inspiration which animate this providential apostolic movement, which fills one of the most beautiful pages in the history of the Church in the United States.

Energies for Latin America

Following immediately on the promulgation of the Second Vatican Ecumenical Council's dogmatic constitution "De Ecclesia," it is most consoling to witness this transfer of energies from one part of the Mystical Body of Christ to another. The Church in your great nation pours forth new, fresh and abundant resources for the "building up the Body of Christ" (cf. Eph. 2, 22; I Cor. 3, 9), and for the preservation and growth of the "People of God" in that neighboring continent.

This brotherly union, this continual multiplication of undertakings, this incessant work of stimulus and coordination, not only give Us great joy, but also supply so many important factors because of their deep doctrinal and pastoral significance.

Thus it is that Our Venerable Brothers share and participate, in a different way to be sure, in Our responsibility and duty as Supreme Pastor of the Flock. They are aware that "qua membra Collegii Episcopalis et legitimi Apostolorum successores, singuli in ea solicitudine pro universa Ecclesia ex Christi institutione et praecepto tenentur, quae, etiamsi per actum iurisdictionis non exercetur, summopere tamen confert ad Ecclesiae universalis emolumentum" (Dogmatic

Constitution De Ecclesia, No. 23). In this way, too, priests feel the call to a wider and more open consideration of their duties towards the apostolic field and the faithful become "ever more aware of their appertaining to the universal Church in which, overcoming the narrow limits of space, they feel engaged all for one and one for all, because they are all sons of the same heavenly Father" (Discourse at the Inauguration of Italian Seminary pro America Latina, Dec. 8, 1964).

True Dimensions of the Church

Today, in fact, it is absolutely indispensable that each person become aware of the true dimensions of the Church, and this greater awareness will lead to a widening of vitality and fuller realization of the meaning of the name Catholic. Whoever enters by Baptism into the great Catholic family shares with all the other members the same unique hope, hears the same appeal, is part of the same body; he enrolls in that "army marching on the road which leads to salvation" (Clement of Rome, Ad Cor. XXXVI, 1); he joins that "great multitude . . . out of all nations and tribes and peoples and tongues" (Apoc. 7, 9).

These considerations, by which We have opened our mind to you, and which could easily be developed at greater length, came to Us spontaneously on reading your report. It is you who have activated their marvelous content by the consoling reality of the facts which you describe therein.

Now, 4,091 in Latin America

The perseverance, continuity and farseeing clarity which mark your labors have had the effect of raising to four thousand and ninety-one the ecclesiastical, religious and lay personnel from the United States now working in Latin America. Nor do We ignore the important fact that in the last two years alone no less than fifty-four diocesan priests, two hundred and ninety-four women Religious and two hundred and eighty-eight lay people have been sent for the first time to that great field of the apostolate, a consoling total of one thousand three hundred and thirty persons.

We send our affectionate paternal greeting to those numerous dioceses which have spontaneously placed at the disposal of the Latin American dioceses a total of one hundred and seventy-nine priests, mostly dedicated to pastoral ministry in fifty-nine parishes entrusted to them in eleven nations of that continent.

Aftermath of Notre Dame

We praise and encourage the Religious communities of men and women which, with perseverance and tenacity, are gradually fulfilling the engagement undertaken at the Congress of Notre Dame, Indiana, in 1961, of offering the Church in Latin America a tithe of their total membership by 1970. They are today represented there by one thousand six hundred and seventy religious priests and lay brothers and by one thousand eight hundred and eighty-three women Religious. In recent years they have expanded existing undertakings, or more frequently have started new initiatives with small groups which are added to little by little, since needs continually increase and demands must be met. While We naturally have special words of praise for those congregations and institutes which have numerically greater representation in Latin America—respecting their modesty We do not mention them by name—yet We cannot forget those hundreds of others which have undertaken the burden of completely new foundations with equal courage and no less sacrifice.

We also express Our sincere appreciation to the hundreds of men and women volunteers, who, with exemplary abnegation, perform their valuable work in many Latin American countries beside the local Catholic organizations.

Commendation for CICOP

Finally, We have learned with pleasure that the United States Bishops' Committee for Latin America has recently established a movement: the Catholic Inter-American Co-operation Program (CICOP), which seeks by educational means to promote greater understanding of Latin America's peoples among the Catholic millions of the United States. We are happy to learn that this year, for the first time, many bishops are introducing this program into their dioceses, and many religious superiors are recommending it to their communities, by advocating the observance of Catholic Inter-American Cooperation Week. Such a step should produce rich fruits of knowledge, warm friendship and Christian concern.

For the Second Annual Conference of the Catholic Inter-American Cooperation Program a theme of great importance and current interest has been chosen. It consists in an analytical inquiry—and We are comforted to learn that representatives of the bishops and laity of Latin America will be associated with you in this work—concerning the social structures of Latin America, in order to determine what is the reality today produced or being produced on that continent, through the rapid substantial changes and continual evolution noted. The conclusions which will be drawn from such study according to the teaching of pontifical documents will indicate the role which the Church must take in that present situation.

Concern for the social situation

Recalling the fact that "Christian social teaching is an integral part of the Christian concept of life" (John XXIII: Encyclical Mater et Magistra, A.A.S., 1961, p. 453), and that "social action also, if properly understood, has its place among the duties of a priest," because "it would be an extension, as it were, of the priestly ministry properly so

called" (Discourse to the Pontifical Commission for Latin
America, July 9, 1963), it is easy to understand the motives
which induce the Church to follow with particular interest,
with apprehension but also with confident expectation, the
evolution of the social situation in Latin America. It is her
mission to give those changes a Christian visage and seal;
to take part in them so as to permeate them with her message of salvation, light and love, which unifies and keeps
united the various social levels and healthy resources of each
people; as it is her duty to ensure the active and operative
presence of her sons in every sector of human activity, and
hence also in the establishment of social conditions in which
the life of all citizens will be lived and developed, as they
reach towards a better, more equitable and more human
future.

More solicitous collaboration

We pray, therefore, that the Second Annual Conference
of the Catholic Inter-American Cooperation Program may
produce many practical results, particularly a wider and
more solicitous collaboration of the United States of America with the Church in Latin America, such as present urgent
needs demand. We laud this specific purpose all the more,
since We are convinced that, in the light of a truly universal
viewpoint, it will not diminish but rather increase the generosity which the American hierarchy, clergy and Catholics
have always shown towards other worldwide activities,
especially the work of the missions, Peter's Pence and the
Papal charities and the aid to needy peoples administered
by your Catholic Relief Services.

Harmonious concord of action with Our Pontifical Commission for Latin America, which has always distinguished
your work in this field of the apostolate, will continue to
guarantee results to your fervid activities. It is in the words
of Saint Paul that We express Our ardent wish: "Qui coepit
in vobis opus bonum, Ipse perficiet" (Phil., I, 6).

In order that divine assistance may guide and sustain your efforts, We assure you of Our prayers, and from Our heart We bestow upon you, Beloved Son, upon the Most Eminent Cardinals, the Most Reverend Archbishops and Bishops, the Congregations and Religious Institutes of Men and Women, and to the Catholic associations of the United States of America, Our affectionate paternal Apostolic Blessing.

From the Vatican, on the Feast of the Epiphany, of Our Lord Jesus Christ, January 6, 1965.

(Signed) PAULUS P.P. VI

INDEX

Act of Bogota, 141
AFL-CIO, 126, 127
Agrarian reform, 111; government, 112
Aid to Latin America—See Church, U.S., aid to Latin America; U.S. aid to Latin America
AIFLD, 123, 130; Social Projects Department, 130
Alliance for Progress, 83, 114, 121, 130, 141, 149, 166
American Institute for Free Labor Development—See AIFLD
Andrés Bello, 55; University of, xi
Arciniegas, German, 42, 44
Argentina, Christian Democracy, 67; education, 197; family, 208
Army, 43, 48
ASAPRESS, Brazilian News Agency, xi
Augustinian Fathers, 174

Bagu, Sergio, 11
Bandeira de Corvalho, Marina, xi, 89
Bedoya Reyes, Luis, 66
Belaunde Terry, Fernando, 66
Bello, Andrés, University of—See Andrés Bello, University of
Betancourt, Romolo, 39, 106
Betancur, Gabriel, 189
Bishops, collegiality, 180
Bishops' Conference, Latin American —See CELAM
Bolivar, Simon, 54, 57
Bolivia, agrarian reform, 113; Christian Democracy, 67; per capita income, 61
Bosch, Juan, 67
Brazil, Basic Education Movement (MEB), xi; Christian Democracy, 66; monarchy, 14; Northeast, Church, 132; Northeast, trade unions, 132; priests in, 173; students, 205

Caldera, Dr. Rafael, xi, 54
Camara, Archbishop Helder, vii

Campos, Alberto, 77
Capitalism, 6, 102, 126
Capitalist liberalism, 94
Cardijn, Joseph Cardinal, 203, 204
Carmelite Fathers, 174
Castro, Cipriano, 104
Castro, Fidel, 54, 82
Catechetical training, 170
Catholic Action, 67, 203
Catholicism, 97, 217
Catholic Relief Services, 175
CELAM (Latin American Bishops' Conference), xii, 99, 201, 220
Center for Economic and Social Development for Latin America—See DESAL
Chaunu, Pierre, 7
Chicago Archdiocese, 174
Chile, Christian Democracy, 66, 201; coalition government, 71; communism, 76; economy, 71; education, Catholic, 171; political structure, 47; students, 201
Christian Democracy, 54, 65, 128, 201; effects of, 69; non-confessional character, 68; principles of, 68; student support of, 69
Christian Democratic Organization of Latin America (ODCA), 72
Christian Democratic Parties, 96
Christian Democrats, World Union of, 73
Christian Family Movement, xiv, 205, 207; statistics, 213
Christian social movements, 89, 202
Church, aggiornamento, 83, 157, 159
Church, Latin American, 18; colonial period, 8; dictatorship and, 49; needs of, 177; progress of, 170; qualities of, 217; social change and, 19, 151, 221—See also pastoral planning; social revolution, the Church's role in; vocations
Church, U.S., 21; aid to Latin America, 121, 234; basic attitudes needed, 182; guidelines for, 175—See also diocesan priests, U.S. in

241